ISBN 0-935038-05-1
ISBN 0-935038-04-3 pbk

Library of Congress Catalog Card Number: 83-80371

Published By
Mana Publishing Co. and Marvin/Richard Enterprises, Inc.
of Honolulu, Hawaii

"When the sun is high in the heavens. . .
look to me.
And by the sign of this flame you will know me. . . .
and my seed after me. . ."

The Chief Iwikauikawa,
who lived in the latter
half of the 16th century.
With this ancestor of King
Kalakaua originated the
custom of burning kukui
torches by daylight on
state occasions.

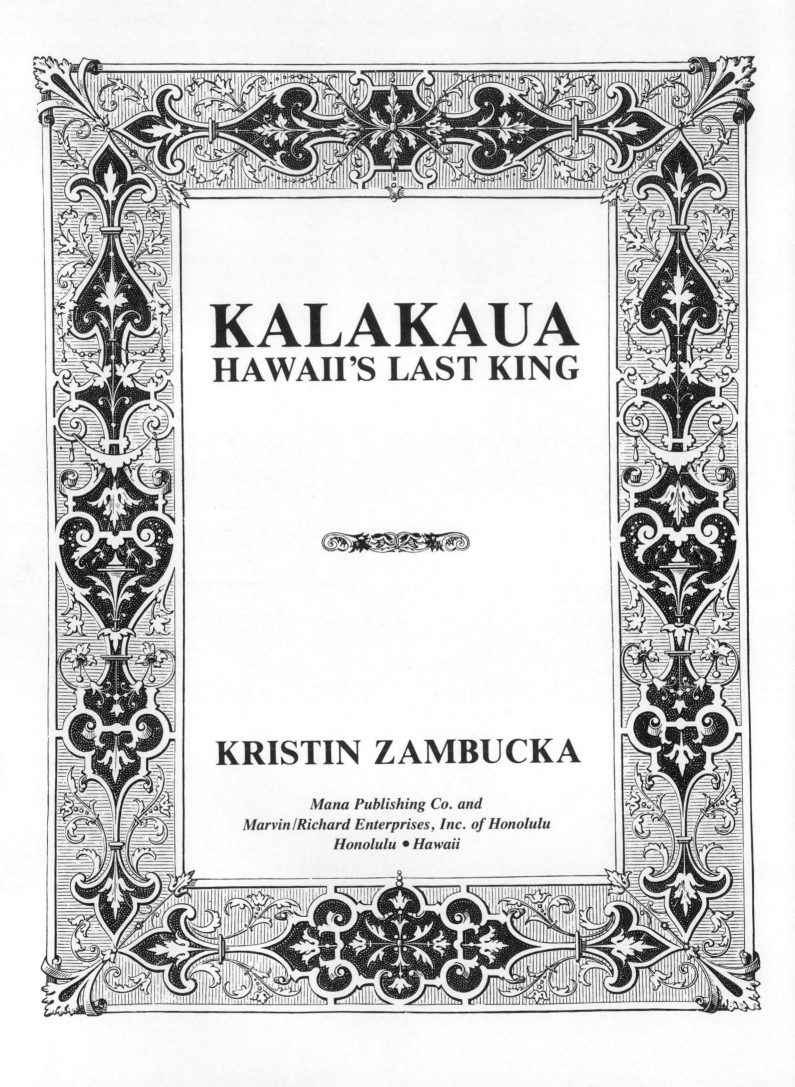

KALAKAUA
HAWAII'S LAST KING

KRISTIN ZAMBUCKA

Mana Publishing Co. and
Marvin/Richard Enterprises, Inc. of Honolulu
Honolulu • Hawaii

Distinguished island families selected their own symbol
of the elements as a mark of their divine origin.
Torrential rain was the symbol of the Kamehamehas.
The makole . . . a blood red mist denoted the Lunalilos.
The founder of the Kalakaua dynasty chose the noonday sun
symbolized by a flaming torch at midday.

"Kalakaua's reign was, in a material sense, the golden age of Hawaiian history. The wealth and importance of the Islands enormously increased, and as a direct consequence of the King's acts. It has been currently supposed that the policy and foresight of the "missionary party" is to be credited with all that he accomplished, since they succeeded in abrogating so many of his prerogatives, and absorbing the lion's share of the benefits derived from it. . . it should, however, be only necessary to remember that the measures which brought about our accession of wealth were not at all in line with a policy of annexation to the United States, which was the very essence of the dominant "missionary" idea. In fact, his progressive foreign policy was well calculated to discourage it. . . "

Liliuokalani, 1898
(from "Hawaii's Story by Hawaii's Queen")

INTRODUCTION

King Kalakaua gained the throne at a crucial time in Hawaiian history. His reign saw the Hawaiian people decimated by illnesses brought to their islands on foreign ships; an alarmingly high infant mortality rate plus the oppression of all things Hawaiian. Meanwhile foreign powers were sniffing at the Palace gates and bolder attempts were made to unseat the King and acquire the reins of government. The most ruthless of these ambitious visitors was a small group of foreign businessmen (comprised mostly of Americans with investments in the Islands) none of whom were or would ever become Hawaiian citizens. They wanted to instil their own civilization and economics. But to secure their hold on the people they had to obliterate all that was Hawaiian. How can you kill a culture and retain a people? King Kalakaua fought these usurpers all the way. So great was his concern that he adopted as his motto *"Ho'oulu Lahui"* (Increase the race). In which direction could he lead his people to save them from extinction? He chose the path back to the old Hawaiian traditions. As a *kahuna* and prophet himself, Kalakaua knew the ultimate fate of the Hawaiians. But although he could foresee it. . . he could do nothing to stop it.

Kristin Zambucka
Honolulu
November 5th, 1982.

Kalakaua 1836 - 1891. In black Military uniform.

An eerie stillness hung over the tree-studded grounds of Iolani Palace. No bird sang, no leaf rustled as the molten sun slid silently down the Western sky.

One by one the old men came. Some were bent like gnarled trees. Others showed astonishingly youthful faces, despite their advanced ages. Tall and erect they held themselves while their years were suspended. Most walked alone across the Palace's crisp, green lawns. A few were accompanied. In many hands could be seen a *kaula hipu'u*, the treasured ball of *olona* cord, knotted at intervals and fingered as a memory device on which were preserved facts and knowledge handed down for generations by word of mouth.

They were the *kahuna* . . . and they came to Honolulu to keep a rendezvous with the reigning King.

Retainers, waiting to admit them to the Palace grew fearful and nervous as they noticed the blood red flash in the eyes of some of these unusual visitors.

When all were finally gathered inside the king's residence, the heavy doors were locked with a snap of metal latches while trusted guardsmen moved to take up their posts solemnly on either side of the doorway.

This was one of many meetings the *kahuna* had with King Kalakaua during the late 1880s.

In the face of severe Missionary antagonism, he called together the few remaining *kahuna* from all the Hawaiian islands, for periodic gatherings. Previously, they had met in secret on the outer islands, but now the King, ignoring the displeasure of the misinformed, openly invited them to Honolulu.

Kahuna kuauhau, the historians; *kahuna lapa'au*, the healers; *kahuna nanauli*, the famous weather forecasters from the Big Island. . . and all other branches of this ancient order were summoned by Kalakaua to pool their knowledge while Hawaiian secretaries faithfully recorded every word.

During this period of the 1880s King Kalakaua established the *"Board of Genealogists of the Hawaiian Chiefs"* and the *"Royal Genealogical Society"* which was limited to members who could prove their noble ancestry by producing authenticated, written genealogies and name chants.

At this time, the *Kumulipo*, the Hawaiian Chant of Creation was also documented (although some scholars claim it was previously recorded in writing as early as 1856.)

In this epic poem the *kahuna* described the creation of the earth and the gods and all living things, and gave an account of a great flood.

Finally they recited the genealogies of 800 generations of Hawaiian Chiefs, stretching back to the time of Umi-a-Liloa (1450-1480 A.D.) from whom King Kalakaua claimed descent. The King was proud of this documented chant and his people considered it one of his strongest hereditary claims to the throne of Hawaii.

On the other hand, the King's enemies accused him of *"hitching his wagon to a star"* or *"trying to establish his divine origin"* by recording the genealogical tables.

A Hawaiian language newspaper, edited by one Kawainui and operated by enemies of the Monarchy, printed by far the wildest story: *". . . Kalakaua is not Hawaiian at all, but the son of a Negro barber. . ."*

The fact was that John Blossom, the *"Negro father"* referred to, had arrived in the Islands when Kalakaua was already a boy of fourteen. Years later, a repentant Kawainui crawled to the King at Iolani Palace and confessed that he had *"taken a bribe"* to print the story.

A witness to the confession, Lot Kamehameha Lane, wanted to kill Kawainui immediately, but the King restrained his friend and forgave the offender, telling him that he understood and thanking him for coming.

During a month's summer visit to Hawaii an eminent German anthropologist, Adolf Bastian borrowed the King's precious manuscript of the *Kumulipo* *". . . the greatest human document known to mankind. . ."* and included excerpts of it in his work, *Die Heilige Sage der Polynesier*, published in Leipzig in 1881. Meanwhile in Honolulu the learned Professor W.D. Alexander, the son of a Missionary and a spokesman for *". . . the good of the community,"* referred to the *Kumulipo* as *". . . vile, obscene and irreligious. . ."* Other vocal enemies of the King chimed in with their dedication to *". . . wipe out all things Polynesian."*

During the periodic meetings of the *kahuna* at Iolani Palace, appointed spies faithfully recorded the name of every visitor and their comings and goings to the King's residence and their imaginations ran riot. *"Kalakaua is reviving heathenism. . ."* claimed *The Gazette*. *"The King is pandering to vice. . ."* The knotted ball of *olona* cord carried by each man was *". . . used in sex orgies. . ."* Enemy newspaper reports continued, dubbing the assembled *kahuna* *"The Ball of Twine Society,"* they stated that *". . . each man would roll the ball towards the lady of his choice . . . then sleep with her."*

Such was the level of their thinking. Such was their misunderstanding of all things Hawaiian.

To explain the astonishing attitude of these Calvinists, a short excursion into history is called for. Their forebears had sprung upon the scene already in the reign of Queen Elizabeth I of England, challenging her authority in Church and State. In the reign of James I small bands of them set out to colonize the New World beginning in 1620 with the pilgrims aboard the *Mayflower*. One of them set the tune by making the following pronouncement:

"The place they had thoughts on was some of the vast and unpeopled countries of America, which are fruitful and fit for habitation; being devoid of all civil inhabitants, where there are only savage and brutish men, which range up and down. . . little otherwise than the wild beasts of the same."

Ignoring the remarks of his detractors, Kalakaua continued his work of preservation. He was the King of Hawaii at a crucial time in Island history and knew the only way to retain Hawaiian sovereignty was to lead his fast diminishing people back to their old traditions.

Rollin Mallory Daggett (appointed U.S. Minister to Hawaii in 1882) wrote down a remark made to him one day by a sad King Kalakaua: *". . . To the Americans we owe our civilization. . . our laws. . . our very form of government. The natives are steadily decreasing in numbers. . . and just as steadily parting with their interests in the soil. There can be but one result. In the end they will lose control of their government as well as of their lands . . . and the Great Republic must then save the people from anarchy by taking the Islands under its protection. . ."*

DAVID LAAMEA KAMANAKAPUU MAHINULANI NALOIAEHUOKALANI LUMIALANI KALAKAUA

David Kalakaua was born on the 16th day of November, 1836 in the city of Honolulu, near the site of the Queen's Hospital. His father was the High Chief Kahanu Kapaakea and his mother the High Chiefess Analea Keohokalole who was a great granddaughter of Keawe-a-heulu, distinguished warrior, confidential councillor and *Kuhina Nui* (Prime Minister) to Kamehameha the Great.

Caesar Kapaakea, Kalakaua's father . . .
a great grandson of Kameeiamoku.

Kalakaua's Mother: The High Chiefess, Analea Keohokaloke

Bishop Museum

Hawaii State Archives

It was the prevalent Hawaiian custom for chiefly children to be adopted by relatives at birth.

From the onset of her pregnancy, it was understood that the expected child of Keohokalole would be adopted by the High Chiefess Liliha, otherwise known as Madame Boki. On learning of this arrangement which was made between Kalakaua's grandfather and Liliha, another Chiefess, Haaheo Kaniu determined to intervene and take the newly born Chief for herself.

Boki and Liliha.

The High Chiefess Haaheo Kaniu waited anxiously at the home of her parents on the night of the expected birth which occurred about 2 a.m. Shortly thereafter, Haaheo took the baby to her own home, *Honuakaha,* one of the residences of the reigning King, Kamehameha III.

Deprived of the baby she had long awaited, Liliha wailed loudly in her disappointment. Nevertheless, for the rest of her life, she took a deep interest in the boy, Kalakaua.

An adept in the art of astrology which she learned from her husband, Boki, Liliha cast Kalakaua's horoscope, predicting that he would *"make his mark in the world. . ."* and further translated from her own words: *". . .From this child, the bones of our ancestors will have life. . ."*

The court of Kamehameha III soon moved to Lahaina, Maui, where Kalakaua remained until he was four years old. The young chief was then taken back to Honolulu to begin his education at the newly founded Royal School under the tuition of Mr. and Mrs. Cooke. Kalakaua was educated at the Cookes' school from 1840 until 1849. As a schoolboy, he was more noted for his sense of fun and humour than for his brilliance as a scholar.

Strong and pugnacious, he would stand up for any cause he believed in, often defending his older, but less robust brother, James Kalokolani, when bullies attacked him.

When the original Royal School broke up, Kalakaua attended Mr. Watts' school at Kawaiahao for a short period until he joined the Royal Day School under the charge of Mr. E.G. Beckwith.

After two months Kalakaua became ill and was forced to leave for Lahaina with his mother.

At the early age of fourteen the future King took his first military instruction from an old Prussian soldier, Captain Franz Funk, whose influence coloured the rest of Kalakaua's life.

Long after, when he became King, he took a great interest in military matters, using German tactics in the training of his own troops.

Miss Sophia Cracroft visiting Hawaii in 1861 with Lady Franklin, wrote of the young Kalakaua: "... *At Kawaihae on the island of Hawaii ... Buckland (Lady Franklin's maid) saw Col. Kalakaua (who is greatly loved by the natives for his amiable character and because he is one of the highest families of pure descent) seated by an old woman with his hands on her shoulders. She had drawn them forward and was kissing first one and then the other with every sign of affection...*"

From: *The Victorian Visitors* by Professor Alfons Korn.

Colonel David Kalakaua.

In 1852, at the age of sixteen, Kalakaua received his first army commission with brevet rank as captain.

He then held the position of first lieutenant in Kapaakea's militia which numbered 240 men.

A year later, Kalakaua began to study law under the Hon. C.C. Harris who was later Chief Justice of the Hawaiian Kingdom.

With his career advancing smoothly, he soon became Military Secretary under W.E. Maikai, then the post of Adjutant General was conferred upon him.

He became a major on the staff of King Kamehameha IV, a member of the Privy Council of State in 1856, and was called to the House of Nobles in 1858. In the same year, Kalakaua joined the Masonic Fraternity (eventually receiving the 33rd degree of that order from General Pike of Virginia in 1874.)

In 1860 David Kalakaua made his first trip abroad accompanying Prince Lot (later Kamehameha V.) They visited the township of Victoria on Vancouver's Island and San Francisco. On his return to the Islands, Kalakaua was appointed third secretary to the Department of the Interior, a position he held until he became Postmaster General in 1863.

When Prince Lot became King (Kamehameha V) in 1865, Kalakaua resigned his position as Postmaster General to become the King's Chamberlain. Two years later he received his first decoration as Knight Companion of the Royal Order of Kamehameha. In 1869 he resigned his post as Chamberlain to further pursue his law studies. In the following year Kalakaua was admitted to the bar.

He was then appointed to a clerkship in the Land Office, a position he held until his accession to the throne in 1874.

David Kalakaua . . . *"before accession."*

Kalakaua greatly enjoyed singing, dancing and drinking with his friends until the small hours of the morning. As a result, he was frequently late for work at the Post Office or he didn't turn up at all, if the party was still going strong. After much criticism about his "irresponsibility", the Minister of Interior wrote to the reigning King, Kamehameha V on March 1st 1865 informing him: *". . . Kalakaua is an unfit man to hold the position of Postmaster General . . . we desire that a change be made, as there are many complaints coming in about the Post Office being badly run etc. . . ."*

Hawaiian Historical Society

Kalakaua on August 7th, 1872 in Honolulu. He was known as *". . . the best dancer in the Islands,"* by those who saw him do the polka.

Kalakaua's inventions.

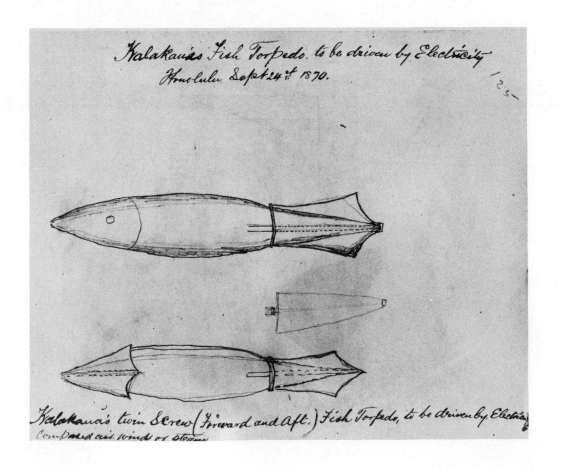

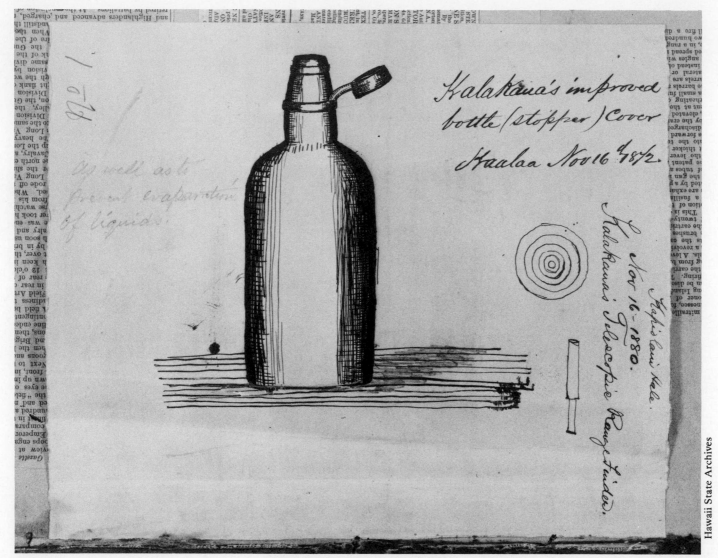

As well as to prevent evaporation of liquids.

Kalakaua's improved bottle (stopper) Cover
Haalaa Nov 16 1872

Kapiolani Kele.
Nov 16 – 1880.
Kalakaua's Telescopic Range Finder.

Another of Kalakaua's inventions.

In a letter dated September 19, 1872, Kalakaua wrote a plea to the Emperor of Brazil for funds to build a vessel he'd invented. He also submitted a request for patronage to Britain's Queen Victoria.

"*. . . I flatter myself,*" Kalakaua wrote. "*Among the inventors of instruments of naval warfare to have invented a submarine torpedo for the destruction of an enemy vessel advancing on a hostile coast. . .*"

He described its effectiveness:

"*. . . The important feature of the invention is the direct action of destruction and the sure annihilation of anything crossing its way . . . I may safely assert that there is nothing afloat with the thickness of iron armour and carrying a plate of three to four inches thick at the ship's bottom . . . save the invention proposed by me and submitted to the British government.*"

On September 26th, 1873 Queen Emma wrote a letter to her cousin Peter Kaeo in which she urged him to follow Kalakaua's example in *"bettering one's self..."* (Taffy was David Kalakaua's nickname):

"...With Taffy's faults we must give him credit for a great ambition ... he has worked and exerted himself both lawfully and to be sure, unlawfully ... to obtain his desire but there is the fact that he has exerted himself ... to secure his coveted object—the Throne ... he has not faltered but keeps on trying ... this is a good point in him which we must copy. He is not idle, he has stumbled and blundered before the public till actually he really has gained courage amongst them and can both speak out and write boldly now..."

J ust before 8:30 on the night of February 3rd, 1874, Hawaii's bachelor king, Lunalilo, died of tuberculosis and alcoholism. That afternoon a reddish mist appeared over the mountain tops and the Hawaiians knew that it signified the death of their king who had been ailing for some time.

As Lunalilo had not named a successor, two candidates now fought for the vacant throne of Hawaii.

One was Queen Emma (the widow of Kamehameha IV) pro-British through blood ties as her grandfather was John Young, British advisor to Kamehameha the Great, whose niece became Young's wife. Queen Emma was also a personal friend of Queen Victoria of England with whom she had visited at Windsor Castle.

David Kalakaua, the other contender, was believed better suited to deal with the world of foreigners into which the small Kingdom of Hawaii had been alarmingly thrust during the 1870s.

Kalakaua in dress suit.

Queen Emma in the 1870's.

Hawaii State Archives

Hawaii State Archives

Writing in the *Republic*, David Adee described Kalakaua as: *"...Hawaiian to the core... but likewise a cosmopolite. A gentleman of education and breeding... suave, intelligent."* The writer continued with his opinion that Kalakaua's diplomacy could *"make an ally of the United States... to get them to protect rather than to seize Hawaii."*

When rumours were being spread that Kalakaua was *"anti-American,"* in fact *" opposed to all members of the white race,"* Kalakaua wrote a letter to the *Advertiser* three months before Lunalilo's death praising the U.S. *"whose leaders had always dealt honourably with the Hawaiian Kingdom."*

King Kalakaua at the White House during visit
to President U.S. Grant, 1874.

Banker Charles Reed Bishop (husband of Bernice Pauahi Bishop) wrote to Hon. Elisha H. Allen on January 20th, 1874:

"...I think Kalakaua has been a good deal misrepresented. Should he have the responsibilities of a sovereign put upon him, I trust that he will be reasonable, impartial and careful. I do not think him prejudiced against any nationality. You and I are aware of his weaknesses and faults, but what can we do, except to make the best of our position..."

While anger was incited during mass meetings held by the supporters of both candidates, Walter Murray Gibson, then editor of the Hawaiian newspaper *Nuhou*, loudly proclaimed his support of David Kalakaua as Hawaii's next ruler: *". . . Contemporary accounts of the campaign do not give the most pleasing picture of Queen Emma. Her intense eagerness to win caused her to say, and to let others say in her behalf, some foolish things. . . and to make some unwise promises. The people of Oahu were deeply stirred by the war of propoganda. On the eve of the election the popular mind was excited to fever heat. . ."*

Marshall William Parke of the Honolulu Police wrote later that *"Emma had promised to free all the prisoners from Honolulu jail, if she were elected. . ."*

Election Day was officially set for February 12th, 1874. At noon the Legislative Assembly met in Honolulu's downtown Courthouse with Governor Paul Nahaolelua presiding.

The courthouse where Kalakaua's 1874 election took place.

Each legislator was given two ballots. Queen Emma's was plain; Kalakaua's was marked with a large black heart on the back.

Outside the Courthouse an excited mob had gathered. Far outnumbering the rest, Queen Emma's supporters from town and country had marched from Nuuanu to the brassy accompaniment of a band.

On reaching the Courthouse they began chanting and singing loudly in praise of their candidate.

At a quarter to three in the afternoon the votes were finally counted. The front door of the Courthouse swung slowly open, and the crowd waited in hushed silence until the results were announced: *". . . thirty-nine votes for Colonel David Kalakaua. . . six for Queen Emma. . ."*

After a moment of shock the crowd went wild and rushed towards the door.

Land Committee members Moehonua, Aholo and Martin Jr. pushed their way through the crowd towards a waiting carriage. They were to carry the news to Kalakaua. . . that he was the winner. But before they could reach the vehicle the angry mob jumped on them. Moehonua was hit with wooden clubs and struck in the head with stones. The other two were quicker and shook themselves free. Their carriage was torn apart as bits of the wreckage were used by the rioters as battering rams to beat their way inside the Courthouse. . . to the native legislators who had *"betrayed Queen Emma."*

Eighty native policemen brought by Marshal Parke to control the mob, were useless. Spectators later reported that most of them seemed to join Emma's supporters.

Marshal Parke

Sanford Dole vainly tried to quiet the surging throng, while one delegate who had voted for Kalakaua was fatally injured when he was thrown bodily from a second story window of the Courthouse.

Once inside the offices, the rioters broke into cabinets, scattered documents, smashed heavy wooden desks, spattered red and black ink around the walls and broke windows. The building's interior was completely wrecked.

No foreigners were attacked, but at least a dozen native delegates were seriously injured: Nahinu, Kipi, Lonoaea, Kaiue. . . Haupu, Kaukaha, Kakani . . . Kupihea, Koakanu, Kuikahi. . . Kupule, Moehonua. . .

William L. Moehonua

Many sought safety hiding behind large cabinets on the top floor of the Courthouse.

Finally, the elected King Kalakaua, the Governor of Oahu; John Dominis, and the Minister of Foreign Affairs, Charles Bishop asked the American Minister Peirce and British Commissioner Wodehouse to bring armed troops ashore.

Two American vessels, USS *Portsmouth* and USS *Tuscarora* had been cruising in Hawaiian waters *"for the protection of American interests during the election."*

One hundred and fifty American sailors and marines scrambled eagerly ashore, joined by seventy British sailors from HMS *Tenedos*.

American guards now cleared the wrecked Courthouse while the British sailors marched to Queen Emma's house in Nuuanu Valley and ordered her frenzied supporters to return to their homes.

At least forty rioters were jailed. American and British troops now stood guard over the Courthouse, the prison, the treasury, the Palace and the barracks.

By evening an uneasy calm had settled over Honolulu and King Kalakaua's reign had begun. The flaming torch was lit. . .

Kalakaua Rex

". . . the germs of many of the evils of Kalakaua's reign may be traced to the reign of Kamehameha V. Under him "heathenism" was revived, evident in the "Pagan orgies" he held at the funeral of his sister, Victoria Kamamalu, in June 1866. . . by his encouragement of the lascivious hula hula *dancers and of the pernicious class of* kahunas *or* sorcerers.

Closely connected with this reaction was a growing jealousy and hatred of foreigners. The reactionary policy of Kamehameha V is well known. . ." From "Kalakaua's Reign: A Sketch of Hawaiian History" by* W.D. Alexander.

Fearing the *"racism"* of which they accused Kalakaua during his campaign when he promised *". . . the increase of the Hawaiian race. . . agricultural and commercial advancement for our people. . ."* eighty local merchants went to American Minister Peirce for *"protection."*

Peirce promptly ordered five American warships to make successive visits to Honolulu *"indefinitely."*

The foreigners were wary of this new king. He was too Hawaiian. At the same time the Hawaiians were wary of the alarming influx of foreigners into the Islands. They saw their way of life and their lands gradually being taken away.

W.D. Alexander

One of Kalakaua's first concerns was the establishment of a line of succession to the throne he now occupied as his marriage was childless.

He appointed his brother, nineteen year old Prince Leleiohoku, as heir apparent.

Kalakaua's two sisters became princesses. Thirty-six year old Lydia Kamakaeha-o-kinau became Princess Liliuokalani (in 1891 she acceded to the throne as Queen Liliuokalani.) She was married to the Governor of Oahu, John Owen Dominis, an American. They had no children.

Twenty-one year old Miriam Auhea was named Princess Likelike. Her husband, Archibald Cleghorn, was a Scot. (In 1875 Princess Kaiulani, their only child, was born to the couple.)

The King's younger sister,
Princess Likelike

Bishop Museum   Hawaii State Archives

The King's sister, Princess Liliuokalani.   Prince William Leleiohoku, Kalakaua's brother

Queen Kapiolani, photographed by M. Dickson in her *"reception dress."*

King Kalakaua's wife Queen Kapiolani was born of the highest ranking chiefs of Kauai. She was a grand-daughter of King Kaumualii. Her three nephews were now designated Princes of Kalakaua's realm. David was named Prince Kawanana-koa, Kuhio became Prince Kalanianaole and Edward's title was Prince Keliiahonui.

Thus King Kalakaua established an undisputed succession and legislative elections to the throne would be unnecessary in the future.

Kalakaua

"Numerous, healthy and industrious. . . this is how I want to see my people. . ."
stated Kalakaua

From a biography of Queen Kapiolani printed in *The Hawaiian Gazette* March 4th, 1874:

"... *King Kalakaua was married twelve years since to Kapiolani, widow of the late Hon. B. Namakeha who was brother of the late Naea, the father of Queen Dowager Emma.*

She is also niece of Keliiahonui, one of the chiefs of Kauai, and was named after Kapiolani, the famous chiefess of Hawaii who broke the "Pele kapu" by making the first descent into the crater of Kilauea in 1824 (as described by Bingham) and who was one of the earliest and most worthy converts to Christianity.

The lady who has thus become elevated to the position of Queen is not only connected with high rank, but is in private life a most estimable woman, and who has been for several years, an unostentatious and exemplary member of St. Andrew's Church of this city.

In his marriage relations, the example of our new sovereign will commend itself to all who deplore the growing tendency of Hawaiians to set them aside, and will doubtless have a good effect on the people of his kingdom."

Kalakaua photographed in New York City circa 1875.

Kapiolani *"in street costume."*

In March 1874, King Kalakaua and Queen Kapiolani set out on the traditional tour of the Islands taken by each new Monarch. Accompanied by a huge entourage, they sailed on the S.S. *Kilauea* for their first port of call, Nawiliwili Harbour on the Island of Kauai.

The Royal Party was rowed ashore on a great surge of song as musicians welcomed them from the shore. Kukui torches blazed in every direction as the King stood on a carpet of flowers and addressed the huge gathering. He spoke of his desire to *"revive the land and its people. . . that we may be restored to our former position of pride and power in our own land."* Kalakaua noticed a large number of children in the audience. *"You are the hope of the nation."* he told them, adding with a smile of encouragement to the parents in the audience to *"have large families."*

The *Kilauea*.

The people could hardly wait for him to finish speaking before they pushed forward to touch their new King.

Old people knelt before him and pressed his hands to their cheeks.

A newsman wrote: *"His Majesty held the people's hearts from that moment. As we circled the Island, everyone who could move followed the King's party. . . ."*

The Royal visitors feasted far into the night at the home of Judge Lilikalani. Throughout the evening people came from all over Kauai with gifts. When Kalakaua and his sister Liliuokalani sang the songs they had composed for the people, the audience responded with tears of joy.

—30—

A glowing fleet of canoes bearing flaming torches and singers sailed out to meet the King as his ship reached the Island of Maui. Bonfires flared along the shoreline until the farthest one flickered out of sight. Every street in Lahaina was lined with flaming kukui torches.

Outside Governor Nahaolelua's home, newsmen recorded the King's address to the people of Maui:

"My people. . . I have come hither to see you as my children. . .that you may look upon me as your father. I desire to incite you toward the renewal of our nation, the extinction of which has been prophesied by some of the foreigners. Shall we sit by and see the structure erected by our fathers fall to pieces? If the house is dilapidated. . . let us repair it. Let us renovate ourselves to the end that the nation may grow again with new life and vigour. . ."

Hawaiian Coat of Arms in Kalakaua's time.

Throughout his tour of the islands, the King frequently addressed his people in their native Hawaiian tongue, urging them to form local branches of *Ho'oulu Lahui* (Increase the Race) a society formed by Kalakaua and Kapiolani to *"restore the prestige of the Hawaiian people..."*

Meanwhile the *"coconut wireless"* (that mysterious telepathic means of communication) was busy sending messages from island to island; descriptions of the new King and his *aloha* for the people.

The *Kilauea* moved on to the Big Island of Hawaii, anchoring in Hilo Bay at midday on April 3rd.

The now familiar burning torches were held aloft in welcome by an excited crowd. Governor Kipi escorted the Royal Party ashore where Kalakaua gave an address remarking that *"these people of the Big Island are among my most beloved children, being of the land of my ancestors..."*

On the fourth day of their tour, the Royal Party sailed for Molokai where the King visited Father Damien and the lepers for more than three hours at lonely Kalaupapa.

Father Damien and lepers at Kalaupapa.

A city street in Honolulu; 1870's.

Heading home at ten o'clock that night, the travellers on the *Kilauea* sighted the glow of Honolulu as huge bonfires burst their golden light along the shore. Hundreds of canoes alight with torches sailed out to greet the returning King. Red and gold fireworks exploded against the night sky over the city while heavy guns boomed a welcome from the dark crater of Punchbowl.

Kalakaua and his Queen walked ashore over a carpet of multi-coloured flowers to the roar of an emotional crowd. Horses, waiting to draw the Royal carriage, were promptly unhitched, and a shouting, singing throng of people pulled the flower-adorned coach all the way to Iolani Palace. Along the way people were holding Kalakaua's symbol: flaming torches. Some waved green palm fronds.

The next day Kalakaua began his tour of Oahu. Wearing their distinctive gourd masks, two members of the sacred order of *Ali'i Mahu* rode out to Makapuu Point to meet the King's Party. Numerous horsemen followed them forming a guard of honour all the way to John Cummins' home at Waimanalo where a great *luau* was awaiting them.

The afternoon was festive with singers and dancers performing for their Monarch while people brought gifts from all over the island.

Residence of J.A. Cummins, Pawaa.

King Kalakaua's tour of his islands was a great triumph. *The Pacific Commercial-Advertiser* remarked: *"The King's royal progress has never been equalled in the islands since the first Kamehameha. In office only two months . . . he has restored the people's confidence. . ."*

In his first public speech King Kalakaua gave the motto for his reign: *Ho'oulu Lahui*. . . (Increase the Race) *"I shall endeavour to preserve and increase the people that they shall multiply and fill the land with chiefs and commoners. . ."*

A strong upsurge of patriotism marked the beginning of Kalakaua's reign. The Hon. Kakina, a legislator from Maui, remarked during the 1875 opening of the Legislature: *"Leprosy and syphilis are foreign diseases. Let us forbid foreigners from coming ashore, and in less than two years, all sickness will disappear . . . and we will again become strong, happy people as in the days of our ancestors. . ."*

Kalakaua

The controversial Walter Murray Gibson owned and edited the Hawaiian language newspaper, *Nuhou*, whose theme was *"Hawaii for the Hawaiians. . ."* Inevitably it was referred to by other merchant-owned newspapers as *"that bastard sheet."*

Editor Gibson dauntlessly called on the new King to make his *". . . a personal rule . . . like the Chiefs of old. Make no concessions to mercenary rings who would shape the welfare of their country to suit their interests. And let there be no terrors of law or religion leading to foeticide . . . such as the Missionary law of moe kolohe under which young parents are imprisoned if the baby comes before the allotted time. Let not officers be pimps of justice to harass Hawaiians in maintenance of a moral standard they cannot understand. Let King Kalakaua have children . . . come how they may . . . to fill his kingdom!"*

The Government's Office Building. Alii-o-lani Hale on King Street.

Eloquent in his first official address, Kalakaua outlined his aims which included: "*. . . no taxes for the parents of large families,*" and "*the Board of Health's increased efforts to preserve the lives of babies.*"

The King continued with his plan for "*a reciprocity treaty*" with the United States. . . and his pre-election promise to fulfill it.

Local sugar planters and businessmen of American, British and German backgrounds had long petitioned the King to "*obtain a reciprocity treaty*" or "*economic disaster*" would befall the Hawaiian Kingdom.

But many could see that if trade were to expand between the United States and Hawaii, Pearl Harbour would have to be ceded to the U.S. Navy for use as a coaling and repair station.

Kalakaua was opposed to any cession of native land. Hoping that reciprocity could be achieved without it, he stated to the Legislature: "*. . . cession of any portion of the national territory is not in consonance with the feeling of the people. . .*"

Hawaiian groups hesitated to accept the idea of any treaty. What if it should lead to American annexation of the islands? Faced with this crucial decision and sensing the enormous changes that would soon engulf his Islands, the King made speeches wherever he could. . . to assure the Hawaiian people that he would "*protect their interests at all costs. . .*"

Pearl Harbour in the 1870's.

In October 1874 Kalakaua sent Chief Justice Elisha H. Allen and Henry Carter (Head of C. Brewer and Co.,) to Washington to commence treaty negotiations.

They were instructed to try to have high standard Hawaiian raw sugar (known in West coast ports as Sandwich Island sugar) admitted to the U.S. "*free of duty*". . . and not to "*enter into any discussions regarding Pearl Harbour. . .*"

A month later King Kalakaua followed his special agents as he sailed on the USS *Benicia* on November 17.

Kalakaua was the first Monarch of any country to visit the U.S. where he was received in Washington by President Ulysses S. Grant on December 15th, 1874.

San Francisco newspapers were enthusiastic about the visit of *"a real king." The Chronicle* described Kalakaua as *"tall and finely formed wearing a suit of black broadcloth of the most fashionable cut."*

The Alta declared *". . . he is a gentleman as well as a king; a well educated, intelligent, popular gentleman. He has the capacity of a statesman."*

The New York Herald reported:

"The King of the Sandwich Islands is a novelty and a prize. His country is sandwiched between America and Asia and is valuable to both continents. To the commerce of the Pacific it is important and especially to America. We interpret his visit as an evidence of good will to the American Nation and it will be our fault if he returns to Honolulu disappointed in his trip. He is no common King, but one to whom we can give our allegiance with a clean conscience for we believe him to be a good man who has the happiness of his nation at heart . . . and a good friend of the American people. Long live King Kalakaua and long may he reign!"

Kalakaua and his Reciprocity Committee in San Francisco at the beginning of 1875. Left to right sitting: John Dominis, Kalakaua, J. M. Kapena. Standing left to right: Henry Peirce, Luther Severance.

Hawaii State Archives

Long discussions followed in the U.S. House of Representatives regarding the wording of the proposed treaty.

By January 30th, 1875 an agreement was reached to *"admit all grades of unrefined Hawaiian sugar, free of duty, to the United States."* King Kalakaua sailed home to a tumultuous welcome on February 15th. Arches bearing messages lined the streets as he rode to the Palace. Most said *"Aloha Kalakaua."*

Back in Washington the Senate voted on March 18th. Only slightly opposed by some sugar growers from the Southern states, the reciprocity treaty was passed by a vote of 51 to 12. The news reached Honolulu on the mail ship *McGregor* on April 14th and a week of celebrations followed.

A new era was ushered in as *"sugar became king."*

The 1875 Legislature opened with great pomp and splendour. Flanked by *kahili* bearers, the King approached Ali'iolani Hale (Government House) on King Street where he spoke from a dais adorned with a unique backdrop . . . the golden feather cloak of Kamehameha the Great.

Princess Kaiulani

1875 was a good year for King Kalakaua. Towards its end a much loved child was born to the Royal Family. The King's sister Princess Likelike gave birth to Princess Kaiulani on October 16th. Delighted with the arrival of his only niece, the King ordered all the bells of the city to welcome her. This child would one day be heir to the throne he occupied.

The year 1876 saw two needs of the growing sugar industry unfulfilled; working capital and cheap labour.

The Reciprocity Treaty with America had provided an excellent sugar market and now the plantations sought loans with which to operate.

Money was provided, once again, by the bountiful hand of the U.S. with loans to the plantations and their agents. Several entrepreneurs brought their own money to invest in sugar. The most prominent was the German-American Claus Spreckels who had already amassed a fortune refining sugar in California. At first opposed to the importing of Hawaiian sugar into the United States, he jumped on the bandwagon once reciprocity was achieved and invested huge amounts in the Hawaiian sugar industry, focussing on Island land, mills and irrigation.

Other names surfaced as the industry developed... Valdemar Knudsen; the son of a Norwegian statesman; James Campbell, an Irishman who had already founded his Pioneer Mill Co., in 1861; Samuel T. Alexander and Henry P. Baldwin, both the sons of Missionary families; Captain James Makee, a whaler from Massachusetts; Heinrich Hackfeld, a German ex-sea captain; Paul Isenberg, another German; and Benjamin Dillingham, an ex-seaman. Fortunes were about to be made in the Hawaiian Islands.

King Kalakaua made every effort to solve the delicate problem of labourers to work the sugar plantations.

He suggested to the 1876 Legislature the "... *building up of the Hawaiian race by a system of bounties given to parents who train up well regulated families...*"

Because of the immediate labour problem, he suggested bringing in other Polynesians from Islands farther south in the Pacific... and perhaps some East Indians.

But Hawaiian legislators objected. They did not want *"any"* foreign labourers imported.

Representative Kakina of Maui boldly stated: *"The Hawaiians would work for the planters if they were paid decent wages. But all they want are slaves... and we are never slaves!"*

On April 10th, 1877, twenty-two year old Prince Leleiohoku died of rheumatic fever. He was heir apparent to his brother's throne.

Thirty-eight year old Princess Liliuokalani (his sister) was appointed heir apparent in his place.

Prince Leleiohoku

Liliuokalani

King Kalakaua sadly observed the dwindling of his race, as another horror spread relentlessly throughout the Islands: leprosy, for which there was no cure.

Taking its toll of the population, it claimed Hawaiians mostly as its victims. *The Advertiser* suggested the Hawaiians' more pronounced *"promiscuity"* was the reason.

By 1879 more than a thousand lepers had been sent to the care of Father Damien in Kalaupapa on the Island of Molokai. Hundreds died there.

Meanwhile, under the pressure of demands from the sugar planters, the floodgates opened and labourers began to flow in from all parts of the world. Between 1877 and 1890 more than 55,000 immigrants poured into Hawaii. Half were Chinese. In 1878 a large group of Portuguese arrived from Madeira and the Azore Islands. It was rumoured that thousands of Japanese would come later.

Brave voices were still heard in the Legislature, as bills were introduced by the Hawaiians: *"Prohibit the sale of lands to foreigners. . . . There must be a penalty for foreigners who engage in business without first taking an oath of allegiance to the King. None but Hawaiians must be admitted to the House of Nobles."*

Portuguese Immigrants.

Hawaii State Archives

Much later . . . The arrival of Japanese immigrants.

Hawaii State Archives

Walter Murray Gibson, Prime Minister from 1882 - 1887.

The much misunderstood Walter Murray Gibson was called a self-serving rogue by many, but none could deny his versatility, nor ignore his charisma. He played many roles: lecturer, political prisoner, rancher, Mormon missionary, businessman, speculator, fluent Hawaiian linguist, prolific writer and newspaper editor. On discovery of Gibson's *"opportunistic"* land purchases on the Island of Lanai, Brigham Young eventually stripped him of all Mormon affiliations. In 1872, a saddened Gibson sailed from Lanai to Honolulu, intent on entering the political arena. The crusader had discovered another *"cause."*

By 1872, *"haole"* diseases had ruthlessly taken their toll of the Hawaiians who now numbered less than a sixth of the 300,000 that Captain Cook estimated in 1778.

Gibson dedicated himself to *'"preservation of the Hawaiian race."* Believing that the people alone hold political clout and voting power, Gibson purchased a newspaper; re-named it *Nuhou* (News), and published it in the Hawaiian language, solely for the natives. *"Hawaii for Hawaiians"* was the paper's theme. By 1878 the political scene was dominated by this outspoken supporter of Hawaiian aims when the controversial *"bearded Messiah"* decided to seek election to the House of Representatives. Despite widespread hatred of Gibson amongst local businessmen who called him a *"racist,"* Gibson stated to an audience of Hawaiians during his 1878 election campaign: *". . . Do not hate the foreigners. Remember instead those among them who guided your kingdom through troubled times in days past, and know that there are those of us today who wish to offer similar service that you may retain your independence. Many of us love you sincerely and wish for your success. . ."*

But *The Hawaiian Gazette* was always wary of the silver-haired orator: *"He (Gibson) got up more special committees, made more reports and by his vanity kept the Legislature in a continual ferment of excitement merely to enable him to air his inordinate ambition to shine as leader of the Assembly and par excellence the special friend and protector general ofthe remnants of the Hawaiian race. . ."*

Once in the Legislature, Gibson's major interest was *"the health of the Hawaiians,"* as measles, smallpox, malaria, syphilis and leprosy knocked down the Islanders at an alarming rate.

Gibson immediately published a manual entitled *Sanitary Instructions for Hawaiians.* It contained simple health rules for the Island people he wished to save. On a moral note, he chided his *"children"* on their *"willingness to co-habit with the diseased* haoles. . ."

Gibson visited Washington, D.C., and Boston to attend to state affairs and for discussions with the eminent sculptor, Thomas Gould, regarding plans for a statue.

The visionary Gibson thought a huge image of Kamehameha the Great should be unveiled in front of Aliiolani Hale on King Street to mark the approaching centenary of Captain Cook's discovery of the Hawaiian Islands in 1778.

During this visit to the mainland, Gibson made an unfortunate acquaintance which he regretted long after. He met the plausible, moustached Italian Celso Caesar Moreno who claimed to be attached to the Italian Diplomatic Legation. Gibson did not bother to check Moreno's credentials, but instead painted a glowing picture of opportunity in Hawaii while chatting in a bar.

In November 1879, who should step ashore in Honolulu but the dashing Italian. He arrived on the China Merchants' Steam Navigation Ship *Ho Chung,* and immediately sought an audience with King Kalakaua.

Moreno's first request was a $24,000 advance to *"establish Hawaii's own steamship line."* He also had plans to lay a cable across the Pacific.

The multi-lingual adventurer captured Kalakaua's attention with his grand schemes and his entertaining companionship to such an extent that his plans for a steamship subsidy and a cable bill were put before the Legislature of 1880. Moreno also had large plans for opium licensing.

All three of Moreno's grandiose schemes fizzled out, but Kalakaua's trust in the Italian appeared dangerous in the eyes of local planters and businessmen. Moreno was being observed with suspicion.

The Advertiser summed up public indignation: *"He has been measured by a discriminating community and their estimate of him is small, notwithstanding his alleged connection with distinguished people of other lands. . . and the public will be heartily glad at the opportunity to bid him an everlasting farewell. . ."*

But Kalakaua liked Moreno and defended him from the barbs of his detractors. On August 14th, the King asked his entire Cabinet to resign. A new Cabinet was named the same day with Celso Caesar Moreno appointed as Minister of Foreign Affairs and Premier.

Bishop Museum

Part of Waikiki where Kalakaua built a home, formerly belonged to earlier royalty, now site of Royal Hawaiian Hotel.

Robert W. Wilcox

There was an uproar in Honolulu. Foreign diplomats announced they would not deal with Moreno, while *"lynching of the Italian"* was openly discussed on the streets of Honolulu, along with *"the prompt abdication of King Kalakaua."*

"Queen Emma should be on the throne!" was the cry at a mass public meeting called to seek the removal of Moreno from office.

Walter Murray Gibson was particularly bitter about the whole situation. He had worked long and hard in support of the King's aims. . . and he felt betrayed when the Italian was given the Premiership of Hawaii after only 274 days in the Islands.

The King held to his appointment of his Italian friend as long as he could in the face of this public outrage. Five days after becoming *"Premier"* Moreno sailed from Honolulu leaving a storm behind him.

In parting Kalakaua gave Moreno *"secret powers"* to discuss plans for Hawaii's neutrality in the U.S. and Europe.

Three part-Hawaiian boys, James K. Booth, Robert Boyd and Robert W. Wilcox, sailed with Moreno to be educated in Italy under his supervision. Later in Kalakaua's reign Wilcox proved to be a prominent revolutionary figure.

On Queen Kapiolani's forty-fifth birthday, December 31st, 1879, the cornerstone was laid for a new Iolani Palace. Before a large group of officials the ceremony was performed with Masonic ritual as King Kalakaua was a 33rd degree Mason.

In an emotional speech, Prime Minister John Kapena remarked on the sacred ground on which they stood: *". . . may it house Hawaiian alii to the end of time. . ."*

Hawaii State Archives

J.M. Kapena — Twice Minister of Finance during Kalakaua's reign.

Hawaii Historical Society

The old wooden Palace of Kamehameha III.

In September 1880, the literary Walter Murray Gibson bought himself another newspaper: *The Pacific Commercial-Advertiser*. (He had already started a bi-lingual newspaper: *Nuhou* in 1873. In his first *Advertiser* editorial he stated: *"The country. . . the whole country is our cause; its people, its society, its health. . . these we will serve with a faithful pen.*

"We will seek to avoid strife. . . but our spirit will not be backward to defend our friends. . . or to condemn any disloyalty to the Hawaiian Throne. We are loyal to the King. . . devoted to the welfare of the people. . . and aim to make this journal an instrument for the advancement and blessing of the Hawaiian nation. . ."

The *Hawaiian Gazette* reported its suspicion that *"Claus Spreckels bought the paper and installed Gibson as Editor. . ."*

In *A Footnote To History* published in 1892, the Scottish writer Robert Louis Stevenson, who made numerous visits to Hawaii and knew both Kalakaua and Gibson, described the relationship between the King and his Prime Minister:

"He (Gibson) was careful to consult the character and prejudices of the late King (Kalakaua). That amiable, far-from-unaccomplished, but too convivial sovereign had a continued use for money. Gibson was observant to keep him well supplied. Kalakaua, one of the most theoretical of men, was filled with visionary schemes for the protection and development of the Polynesian race. Gibson fell in step with him; it is even thought he may have shared in his illusions or inspired them. . ."

Kalakaua's Waikiki Residence.

On a hazy morning in January, 1881, King Kalakaua sat talking with his Attorney General, William N. Armstrong, on the *lanai* of the King's country home at Waikiki. Thoughtfully watching the surf as it foamed over the coral reef, the King remarked that his *"troubles were over"* and he could now plan the world trip he had long considered. There were many reasons to explore the vast world outside his isolated Islands. He would personally look into the crucial question of immigration. Furthermore it was time Hawaii took her rightful place beside the other nations of the world. Kalakaua would study the royal courts of Europe for many answers.

During his six years on the throne, Kalakaua had suffered his share of difficulties with some *"foreign subjects"* who held much property and power in the Hawaiian Kingdom. They were extremely outspoken through their interests in Honolulu's major newspapers, often threatening *"insurrection"* because of *"King Kalakaua's political errors."*

But the King always yielded to their demands. . . eventually. During a lull in the storm following the devastating Moreno incident Kalakaua had entertained 100 of these *"subjects"* at a huge banquet just the night before he reached his decision to make his world trip.

Kalakaua's project was approved by the Cabinet and Privy Council: funds were provided for the trip and his travelling companions were chosen; Attorney General William N. Armstrong was newly entitled *"Royal Commissioner of Immigration."* He was given instructions to *"seek over the world. . . recruits to the depleted population of the Kingdom. . ."*

The King's Chamberlain, Colonel Charles H. Judd, was chosen as the other official and the third companion was a constant *"thorn in the side"* of the other two proper sons of Protestant missionaries. Kalakaua selected his personal valet, Robert, a frequently drunken German with a chequered past.

Robert had arrived in Honolulu as a ship's cook and soon became employed as the King's chef. But he insisted that he was really the Baron von Oehlhoffen suffering from *"reduced circumstances."*

Obviously the German was an educated man. Noting also that he was a brilliant linguist, Kalakaua made him pledge sobriety as he considered him *"useful"* on the trip despite the many protests from the two official travellers, Armstrong and Judd.

After it was announced that the King was leaving, groups of Hawaiians gathered in the Palace grounds, filling the nights with their songs of farewell and safe return.

Kalakaua gave many speeches explaining to the people his reasons for making the long journey: *". . . so that we may become a strong, secure and independent people."*

Princess Liliuokalani was named Regent in the King's absence, while Queen Kapiolani supervised the packing of her husband's luggage, carefully wrapping the Royal Standard in canvas and including an ancestral feathered cloak. Draped with sweet smelling vines of *maile,* Hawaiian singers and dancers performed all day and all night in praise of their King, until the Royal Party sailed on the steamer *City of Sydney* which had arrived late to pick them up.

At dawn on January 21, 1881, the King and his suite, draped with flower leis, sailed toward San Francisco.

The moving strains of Hawaii Ponoi, played by the Royal Hawaiian Military Band followed them out of the harbour.

Kalakaua's intention to *"travel incognito"* was forgotten when the ship's captain requested the King's permission to fly the Hawaiian Royal Standard as they entered San Francisco harbour. They were greeted by a twenty-one gun salute as the city opened its arms to a *"real King"* as it had done six years before.

On the 4th of March the King's Party steamed into the Bay of Yeddo by the first light of dawn.

Kalakaua was the first King of a western, Christian nation to ever visit Japan and Emperor Mutsuhito was lavish in his hospitality.

The visitors were given the use of a palace surrounded by a moat with numerous attendants at their service.

It was during this visit to Japan that King Kalakaua proposed the betrothal of his niece, Princess Kaiulani, then five years old, to a young Japanese prince, fifteen year old Prince Yamashina Sadamaro, a naval cadet who was attached to Kalakaua's staff as Naval Aide-de-Camp for a day. Kalakaua wrote in his diary his most favourable impression of the boy: *". . . he is a lively, young, very bright, intelligent and promising lad. . ."*

(In early 1882 two polite letters from Foreign Minister Inouye Kaoru and the Prince himself declined the offer of marriage to a Hawaiian Princess *"as the Prince was already betrothed."* Japan at that time also refused to send immigrants to Hawaii.

The young Princess Kaiulani.

Prince Yamashina Sadamaro.

Bishop Museum

Emperor of Japan, 1881.

Hawaii State Archives

King Kalakaua in Japan, 1881. Left to right, front: Lieut. Gen. Prince Yoshiaki, Kalakaua, Minister of Finance Yoshii Amatami. Standing at back: Left to right. Judd, First Secretary of Finance Riyosuke Sugai, Armstrong.

The Royal Party moved on through China, Siam and India. On reaching Egypt they were shown great hospitality as Tewfik, the Khedive (also the Viceroy) instinctively understood the problems of the Hawaiian King. The Egyptian Khedive had long been tired of European dominance in his own country. In Alexandria, Kalakaua addressed the Masonic Fraternity, astonishing its members with his knowledge of their ancient order and Egyptian history.

Bishop Museum

The Viceroy of Egypt, 1881.

Col. C.H. Judd, Kalakaua's Chamberlain.

Pope Leo XIII

In Italy, a disturbing figure from the past turned up again to annoy the travelling *"officials,"* Mr. Armstrong and Mr. Judd (they had enough to put up with already with Valet Robert's several drunken sessions, just as they had predicted).

As their ship anchored at Naples, the colourful Celso Caesar Moreno bounced on board accompanied by the Mayor of the city and an Italian Admiral.

Judd and Armstrong watched horrified as Moreno *"took charge"* of the King and whisked him off to a nearby hotel. Kalakaua was still intrigued by the Italian's schemes for Hawaiian expansion. During their ill-fated friendship in Hawaii, Moreno had talked of obtaining a huge loan from China plus the arrangement of immigration on a vast scale from that country, of establishing Hawaii's own steamship line, and of ultimately wresting the power from the missionary and foreign influences that dominated the King's Government. Listening with interest to Moreno, Kalakaua liked the idea of being independent.

Before leaving Italy, Kalakaua was presented to King Umberto and Queen Margherita and had an audience with Pope Leo XIII.

The touring suite left for England via Paris. Throughout the trip efforts continued to recruit immigrants for Hawaii. The King wanted *"permanent settlers"* for the Islands, but Mr. Armstrong's attitude was criticized back home in Hawaii where *The Advertiser* noted: *"Armstrong is obviously endeavouring to hinder any immigration except that of cheap plantation labour... although his instructions from the King are that he is to bring families for re-populating the Islands..."*

In Germany, the Hawaiian King's interest in military matters was revived. At Potsdam he was greatly impressed by the uniforms and army manoeuvres of 7000 mounted troops, a display arranged in his honour by Prince William of Prussia.

In England, Queen Victoria received Kalakaua at Windsor Castle and invited him to explore the huge building's interior. Her Majesty expressed amazement at the Hawaiian Monarch's easy command of the English language. She was told he had learned it as a child from the Missionary Schools in Honolulu. Victoria said she hoped Kalakaua would enjoy his visit to England as she had always been interested in his far-off kingdom, having learned about it during a visit to Windsor Castle by Queen Emma some years before.

Claridges Hotel, London . . . as it was when King Kalakaua stayed there in 1881.

Queen Victoria of England, 1881.

Extract from Queen Victoria's Journal for July 11th 1881: "... *After luncheon, went with my children and grand children, to the Green Drawing Room, where I received King Kalikaua (sic) of Hawaii, who was presented by Lord Granville. He was accompanied by his two gentlemen & Mr. Synge who is attached to him! King Kalikaua is tall, darker than Queen Emma, but with the same cast of features, black but not woolly hair, more like the New Zealanders, but without their thick lips. He is very gentlemanlike & pleasing & speaks English perfectly; he is of course a Christian. I asked him to sit down after presenting my family & his gentlemen were then presented to me...*"

In all the European capitals King Kalakaua was received with courtesy, respect and interest.

One of his travelling companions, William Armstrong, later expressed his rather biased opinion in his book, *Around The World With A King*

"*. . . The extinction of Kalakaua's Monarchy was due to the cold and inexorable law of political evolution. . . The King did not understand this law of evolution. He did not see that his monarchy was indulgently tolerated by the Anglo Saxons so long as it did not put in jeopardy their rigid ideas regarding the rights of persons and property and the administration of law. . .*"

Soon after the Royal travelling party returned to Hawaii, Armstrong resigned his post in Kalakaua's Cabinet in protest against *"the King's elaborate, expensive and useless plans for a coronation."*

Kauikeaouli Gate (King Street entrance to Iolani Palace) decorated in honour of Kalakaua's return from his world trip, October 29th 1881.

William L. Green

In the four month period between December 1st, 1880 and April 2nd 1881 more than 4,400 Chinese came ashore in Honolulu. Some of the ships concealed numerous cases of smallpox on board until the first week in February saw an epidemic raging throughout Oahu. *"The disease seems to go through our native population like a fire. . ."* wrote a distraught Minister of Foreign Affairs, William Green. For six months smallpox ravaged the Islands. The number of reported cases totalled 797 (including some on Kauai). 287 people died, mostly Hawaiians.

Almost $100,000 was authorized by the Cabinet as an *"emergency expenditure."* Nevertheless, Premier Green's Ministry and the Board of Health were attacked for their *"poor management of the situation."*

A saddened King Kalakaua newly embarked on his round-the-world trip, was informed of the alarming toll being taken of the native population back home. He expresses some of his exasperation in letters to his sister Liliuokalani.

From Cairo, Egypt, June 21, 1881:

"My Dear Sister,

I am glad to hear everything is going on well. I see by the papers of your performing your duties faithfully. As you are a religious and praying woman, Oh! All the religious people praise you! But what is the use of prayer after 293 lives of our poor people have gone to their everlasting peace. Is it to thank him for killing. . . or is it to thank him for sending them to him or the other place. Which I never believed in the efficacy of prayer and consequently I never allowed myself to be ruled by the Church members to allow a thanksgiving prayer to be offered to God for the good of the Nation. . . for in my opinion it is only a mockery. The idea of offering prayer when hundreds are dying around you. To save the life of the people is to work and not pray. To find and stop the causes of death of our people and not cry and whine like a child and say to God: "that it is good oh Lord that those it hath visited know thus. . ."

And further to Liliuokalani written from Claridges Hotel, Brook St, W. July 12, 1881:

". . . The Queen (Victoria) was announced and all in the room made a very low and gracious bow. I made a most profound one. And another. She came up to me and took my hand and then sat on a sofa asking me to sit down on a chair facing the sofa near her. All the gentlemen of the Court stood in perfect silence when the conversation took place between Her Majesty and myself. She said that I was making a very long tour. I answered very fluently giving her very nearly in detail a description of our voyage. Then I said I regretted not meeting the Duke of Edinburgh . . . or rather she began first and mentioned that her son often mentioned my name. . . She then asked of Queen Emma and I told her she was very well and saw her a day before we left. This is only a few remarks I can remember for I was quite electrified and monopolized the whole of the conversation that took place during the interview. She asked particularly where I learned English. . . as my accent was perfect. . .

Ua lio pelekane loa au kaia wa. . . lio pelekane loa iho la au ia wa a pela no a nanei la ke hoi aku au (I have become very British at this time . . . and I am still, now that I am going away. . .) (sic)

I replied that I was educated in the same school as Queen Emma and all the Royal Kings and Princesses of our country. She then asked me to present her daughter HRH Princess Louise and Princess Beatrice and other members of her family. . ."

Kalakaua wrote again to his sister Liliuokalani from the Continental Hotel, Paris, August 10, 1881, describing his recent visit to Vienna and his opinion of churchgoers:

"... A ladies' band is playing every evening in full blast when Vienna is alive at the Pratta... some listening... some sitting around beer tables, some dancing and such enjoyment. Thereafter operas, racing and general holiday. The Jews' stores and warehouses all opened. Churches too going on at the same time without a disorder or disturbance to be heard among a population of over a million. Can it possibly be that these light hearted happy people are all going to H- -ll? All enjoying Nature as Nature's best gift? Surely not! But what a contrast to our miserable, bigoted community. All sober and down in the mouth... keeping a wrong Sabbath instead of a proper Sunday. The pure are so pure that the impure should make the Sunday a day of mockery with such rubbish trash that we have so long been lead to believe, it is a wonder that we have not risen any higher than the common brute..."

Hawai State Archives

Kapiolani photographed by A.A. Montano.

QUEEN KAPIOLANI (1834 - 1899)

As part of her life's work for the society HO'OULU LAHUI (Increase the Race), Queen Kapiolani founded Kapiolani Maternity Home to assist Hawaiian mothers. Later whe willed her large personal fortune for the hospital's future maintenance *"so that the babies may live."* She also opened the Kapiolani Home *"for girls born of leprous parents"* in 1885.

In his despatches of September 20th, 1882, the U.S. Minister, Rollin M. Daggett, described the four groups who opposed King Kalakaua and his Ministry:

"(I) A very considerable native population who question King Kalakaua's right to the throne. This element favours Queen Emma. . . however this is not a dangerous element politically, for the natives can no longer be regarded as a controlling physical force in the Hawaiian Kingdom.

(II) The Annexationists, composed principally of young Americans, the most of them with no great property interests in the Islands. They do not number perhaps more than three or four hundred in the Islands, but are zealous and outspoken. The most of them favour the abrogation of the Treaty of Reciprocity, believing that the large sugar interests of the Islands principally in the hands of Americans and fostered by the Treaty, would in the event of abrogation, be forced to seek relief from disaster in annexation. . .

(III) American and European planters and property holders. Their opposition however, is less to the form of government than to the manner of its administration. They charge the King with extravagance, and the Ministry with doing less than their duty in submitting to it. This is a wholesome opposition and carries with it no menace to the stability of the government.

(IV) Americans who have been either relieved from service under the government or who would be willing to accept profitable public positions held by others. This class includes what is known as the "Missionary Influence."

The Legislative session of 1882 was a stormy one during which lack of confidence in the current Ministry was loudly expressed. British Commissioner Woodehouse wrote in his despatches: *"The Cabinet is thoroughly disorganized . . . the antagonistic elements being Mr. Green, Premier and Foreign Minister . . . and Mr. Armstrong, Attorney General and acting Minister of the Interior. . ."*

On May 8th Premier Green wrote to the Minister of the Interior, H.A.P. Carter *". . . I, this morning. . . made up my mind to resign. . . things have got a little mixed. . . "* On May 18th, Attorney General Armstrong followed suit with the entire Cabinet resigning office on May 19th.

At this time of turmoil the controversial Walter Murray Gibson saw his fondest dream materialize: the King offered him the Premiership of Hawaii plus the portfolio of Foreign Affairs. To no one's surprise Gibson accepted.

King Kalakaua immediately asked Gibson to form his new Ministry whose names were announced on Saturday, May 20th: Walter Murray Gibson, Premier and Minister of Foreign Affairs; Simon Kaloa Kaai, Minister of the Interior; John Edwin Bush, Minister of Finance; Edward Preston, Attorney General. Bearers of flaming torches marched that night in procession to celebrate the new political regime.

"Equal Rights At Last!" one banner proclaimed.

In the five years between 1882 and 1887 King Kalakaua repeatedly changed his Cabinets but Walter Murray Gibson always held on. While other Ministers came and went, with all the accompanying storms, Gibson occupied each Cabinet post, sometimes managing several at the same time.

On June 23rd, 1882, British Commissioner James H. Wodehouse wrote to Lord Granville (British Foreign Minister in 1880) remarking on Gibson's Cabinet:

". . . It would have been difficult, if not impossible for Mr. Gibson who has always fostered the Hawaiian element, to have formed a Cabinet without two Hawaiians in it. . . and Mr. Kaai although very unscrupulous and very unreliable has always had great influence with the natives, and would have been a very dangerous opponent. The same remarks will apply to the selection of Mr. Bush as Minister of Finance and who is moreover a very intimate friend of the King's. The Attorney General, who has been in office before, is a very able lawyer, but is indolent, and the whole burden of carrying on the Government will really be borne by the Premier. . ."

Hawaii State Archives

Simon K. Kaai, Kalakaua's Minister of Finance 1878, Minister of the Interior 1882, Minister of Finance 1882.

In her book *This Life I've Loved* Isobel Strong wrote that she learned to her surprise that the word "Missionary" had a political significance like Democrat or Republican. The leaders were the sons and grandsons of the original missionaries who came to Hawaii to convert the heathen. By the 1880's they were rich, prosperous American businessmen.

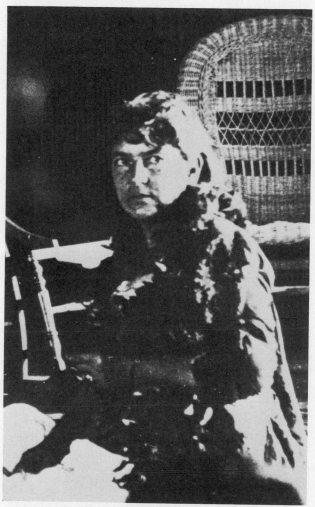

Isobel Strong. Her mother and stepfather, Robert Louis Stevenson arrived later for an Island sojourn.

Quickly learning that there were two distinct social sets in Honolulu, the Royal Party and the Missionary Group, Isobel Strong and her husband, Joe decided to join the Royalists. But not before she had heard *"gossip"* from both sides: *". . . the Missionaries now owned most of the land that once belonged to the natives. . . that the wealth of many of them came from barrels of oil their fathers had begged from the Yankee whalers for mission work. . . and later sold for their own profit. . . and many tales of that kind. On their side the Missionary ladies told me the King was a drunkard and a spendthrift, the son of a Negro barber and not fit to rule a nation. . . and I was warned against the fast set that surrounded him. Feelings at this time ran high, and neither faction used any restraint in the stories they told of the other . . ."*

Iolani Palace, shortly after completion, 1882. Grounds being developed. . . flag poles not yet on towers.

Major Leleu Kinimaka in command of The King's Own Guards, Iolani Palace, May 3rd, 1882.

With completion of the new Iolani Palace late in 1882 Kalakaua decided to stage his coronation on the ninth anniversary of his accession to the throne: February 12, 1883. The financial legislation of 1882 caused an uproar of protest from the newspapers and business community with special bitterness voiced towards expenses appropriated for the planned coronation.

At first only $10,000 was allotted, but the amount spent far exceeded $50,000 by the time the ceremonies were over. The U.S. Minister, Rollin Daggett, commented: *"the Coronation expenses would find partial compensation in a temporary increase in trade and the general gratification of the native population. Not that King Kalakaua is a universal favourite with his own people, but that the average native is willing to sacrifice almost any sentiment to that of display. . ."*

The pavilion decorated for the Coronation, Feburary 12th, 1883.

The bandstand, *"Keliiponi Hale,"* was first built as the central platform for the coronation of King Kalakaua and Queen Kapiolani. Originally erected in front of the King Street steps of the Palace, it cost $9,000 and was surrounded on three sides by a large amphitheatre which provided seats for the Coronation guests. Only the royal family entered *"Keliiponi Hale"* on this occasion, and it was moved to its present location following the Coronation ceremony.

In Kalakaua's time the Royal Hawaiian Band often played in the bandstand, and the structure served as a stage for royal functions too large to be held within the Palace. Many *luaus* and grand balls were held in an enormous tent erected beneath the trees that stood between *"Keliiponi Hale"* and the Palace, while at other times the same grounds served as the royal croquet court.

The Coronation of Kalakaua.

Bishop Museum

The coronation ceremony was scheduled for noon, but by 9 a.m. the amphitheatre was crowded to capacity with more than 4000 others spilling over; their clothing adding bright patches of colour to the palace lawns.

At eleven-fifteen, conch shells were blown to herald the opening of the ceremony. The King's Chamberlain, Charles H. Judd, appeared in the doorway of the Palace and came slowly down the walkway towards the Pavilion. Next came John Kapena (Marshal of the Household), W.C. Parke (Marshal of the Kingdom), Godfrey Rhodes (Legislative President), the Rev. Alexander Macintosh and Chancellor A. Francis Judd (Chief Justice).

Princess Liliuokalani wore a gold brocade dress with a train and a headdress of gold leaves and white feathers. Princess Likelike wore white satin brocade trimmed with pearls and ostrich feathers.

Queen Kapiolani's sisters, Poomaikelani and Kekaulike, both wore red velvet gowns with long trains. As the King and Queen appeared in the Palace doorway, a murmur of excitement arose from the crowd.

Hawaii State Archives

above
Queen Kapiolani in Coronation dress.

left
Princess Kekaulike, sister of Queen Kapiolani.

right
Princess Poomaikelani, sister of Queen Kapiolani.

Hawaii State Archives

Hawaii State Archives

—68—

The Crowns

Isobel Strong recalls Coronation Day:

"It was a glorious day, sunny and vivid with that cool breath of the sea that makes the climate of the Islands so perfect. The Coronation itself was held in the garden of the palace under a pavilion. My memory of it is a blaze of colour, crowds and heat. We were too far away to see much more than the pantomime, the King and a group of dignitaries going through a ceremony of some kind that ended in Kalakaua placing the crown on his own head. There was a burst of applause from the crowd; the Royal Hawaiian Band played the national anthem, Hawaii Ponoi; the King and his party walked back to the palace and it was all over. . ."

And later, writing of the Coronation Ball which she attended at Iolani Palace:

". . . King Kalakaua was a strikingly fine looking man in a resplendent uniform of white and gold which his good figure set off to advantage. Beside him stood Queen Kapiolani, tall and very stout. She was dressed in rich velvet with the latest cut, a style most unbecoming to her. She was very serious and I seemed to see in her dark face an expression of timidity and appeal. Of pure Hawaiian stock, descendant of a long line of chiefs, she had never learned to speak English. I think she was a little afraid of the Americans coming in such numbers to her country. She may have had a premonition of the future awaiting Hawaii. . ."

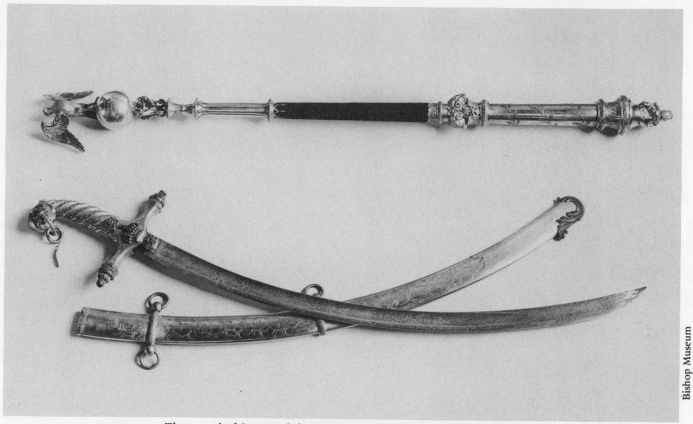

Bishop Museum

The sword of State and the sceptre used in Kalakaua's Coronation.

Gibson's thoughts were that ". . . *the Coronation was a measure long contemplated by Hawaiian sovereigns in imitation of the custom of European monarchical states. The native ceremony of the Poni . . . or an anointment, had in former times been practised by the chiefs, but it was deemed desirable that the more modern and Christian rite should be celebrated. . .*"

Later, Queen Liliuokalani wrote of the Coronation in her book, *Hawaii's Story by Hawaii's Queen*": ". . . *There was a serious purpose of national importance; the direct line of the Kamehamehas having become extinct, it was succeeded by the Keawe-a-Heulu line, its founder having been first cousin to the father of Kamehameha I. It was wise and patriotic to spend money to awaken in the people a national pride. . .*"

Honolulu was deluged by heavy rains for three days prior to Coronation Day. But ". . . *on the morning of the 12th, the sun shone forth with unwonted brilliance. . .*" The Advertiser reported. "*And strange to say, the morning star was seen in the heavens shining contemporaneously with the sun. . .*"

Kalakaua wore the white uniform of the King's Guards, white helmet with a red, white and blue plume, plus many Royal decorations clustered on the front of his jacket: the Grand Cordon, Star and collar of the Order of Kamehameha, and decorations from the imperial courts of Austria, Germany, Japan, England, Portugal and Siam. Kapiolani wore a gown of red cardinal velvet with an ermine border and a white satin front panel embroidered in gold. She carried a fine lace fan.

As the crowd pushed forward for a better view, bearers carefully carried the regalia with which the King was to be invested, a combination of ancient Hawaiian and modern European.

The golden feather cloak of Kamehameha the Great (made from an estimated 450,000 feathers of the o'o bird) was carried towards the Pavilion; then came the seven foot tusk of narwhal, the *Pulo'ulo'u* (the Tabu stick), the *Palaoa* (whale's tooth), the sacred torch of Iwi-kau-ikaua and the Royal *kahilis*; symbols of Hawaiian Chieftainship.

Throne Room, Iolani Palace.

King Kalakaua

Then came the sword of state, the sceptre and ring followed by the two crowns borne on satin cushions by Princes David Kawananakoa and Jonah Kuhio Kalanianaole. Diamonds, opals, pearls, emeralds, rubies and golden taro leaves glistened around the base of each crown.

Envoys from Japan, Britain and the United States beside diplomats representing the German Empire, Austria, Hungary and other European countries watched as the ceremony began. Meanwhile, two American warships, the *Lackawanna* and the *Wachusetts* were anchored in Honolulu Harbour beside the British ship HMS *Mutine* and the French corvette *Limier*. They had been ordered to keep watch on the city in case a disturbance erupted.

Meanwhile, the voices of the choir rose to the tune of *"Almighty Father Hear! The Isles do wait on thee."* Marshal Kapena recited the King's genealogy after which Princess Poomaikelani (sister of the Queen) presented the Hawaiian regalia to the King. Chief Justice Judd administered the oath and Kalakaua had the sword of state (the ensign of justice and mercy) placed in his hands. Princess Kekaulike, another sister of the Queen, held the Royal mantle (the ensign of knowledge and wisdom) which was placed on the King's shoulders. The ring (the ensign of kingly dignity) was placed on the fourth finger of the King's right hand. Finally, Chancellor Judd handed Kalakaua the sceptre (the ensign of kingly power and justice).

Prince Kawananakoa and Prince Kalanianaole moved forward bearing the crowns while the choir sang louder this time: *"Almighty Father! We do bring gold and gems for the King..."*

The climax of the ceremony brought a hush to the crowd. Godfrey Rhodes, President of the Legislative Assembly, held the King's crown aloft for the people to see... then handed it to Chancellor Judd who addressed King Kalakaua: *"Receive this crown of pure gold to adorn the high station wherein thou hast been placed."*

In a gesture that has been much misunderstood, Kalakaua then crowned himself as no one else in the kingdom possessed *mana* high enough to enable him to touch the king's head.

Kalakaua then placed the smaller crown on the head of his Queen, Kapiolani, saying: *"I place this crown upon your head to share the honours of my throne."*

As the Royal couple knelt, the Rev. Macintosh recited a prayer. The King and Queen then took their seats and a salvo of guns boomed from a battery on the shore, followed by a resounding volley from the warships anchored in the harbour.

The choir sang joyously now the hymn composed by Prime Minister Gibson especially for the event: *"Cry Out O Isles With Joy!"*

Kalakaua's Coronation Day was surprisingly peaceful. The expected riots did not rock the town and Gibson was not assassinated, although it had been widely rumoured that he would be *"shot down on Coronation Day."*

The City of Honolulu dressed itself up and celebrated the Coronation for two weeks.

On February 14, in heavy rains, King Kalakaua unveiled the bronze statue of Kamehameha I in front of Aliiolani Hale across the street from Iolani Palace.

A dazzling display of fireworks burst into the night sky of February 17. Three days later the Coronation Ball was held at Iolani Palace. Surprising his guests, Kalakaua had the throne room lit by electricity for the first time.

A regatta dotted the harbour with sailboats and craft of all shapes and sizes two days later, while crowds enjoyed the excitement of horse racing at Kapiolani Park on February 26. Hula dances were held each night in the Palace grounds and a huge *luau* catered to 5000 hungry guests for an entire afternoon.

Meanwhile, *The Pacific Commercial-Advertiser* published colourful reports of the Coronation festivities. Other newspapers were not so complimentary of the *"King's Day."* The Planters Monthly declared *". . . the so-called Coronation of the King. . . with the attendant follies and extravagances, has been directly damaging to the property interests and welfare of the country. It has been demoralizing in its influence. . . and productive only of harm. For the furtherance of the Coronation, public measures of pressing importance have been neglected. . ."*

Another *"opposition"* paper, *The Hawaiian Gazette*, was particularly scathing about the staging of hula dances calling them*". . . the very apotheosis of grossness. . ."* while a local attorney, W.R. Castle, almost in a faint after having the Hawaiian words translated from the hula program, went so far as to bring charges of obscenity against one of Kalakaua's aides and the printer of the program.

The King's *"offensive"* Hula program is reproduced in part at the end of this book.

Revival of hula. . . popularity of guitar.

Ukulele's popularity during Kalakaua's reign.

Ancient Hawaiian *meles* or chants have always honoured various parts of the human body. The accused printer, Robert Grieve, claiming complete ignorance of the Hawaiian language, said he did not know what he was printing. He was fined by the Court, but on appeal his conviction was reversed.

Later, ex-Cabinet Minister W.D. Armstrong who had travelled around the world with King Kalakaua in 1881, thought he had the last word in dubbing the Coronation "*. . . this grotesque pageantry of white washed paganism.*"

American newsman, David Graham Adee wrote his observation of the Hawaiian people in 1883:

"*. . . born in a land that ordered them tranquil of mind and indifferent to acquisition. . . they were unable to cope with an aggressive, avaricious and self-assertive civilization.*

"*Calvinism broke down their spirits. . . as European garments broke down their health.*"

Poet Charles Warren Stoddard wrote of Kalakaua:

"Oh what a King he was! Such a King as one reads of in nursery tales. He was all things to all men; a most companionable person. Possessed of rare refinement, he was as much at ease with a crew of 'rollicking rams' as in the throne room."

The King in Military Uniform.

A rare old photo of Kalakaua at his desk in Iolani Palace, 1883. The King's office was also known as the Library where he signed all public documents including railroad franchises. The only portrait ever made of the King at work, shows the telephone on the wall behind him near the door. Sitting left to right: C. O. Berger, Sam Parker, Kalakaua at desk. Standing: John Baker (left), Sam Nowlein (right).

Always an innovator, Kalakaua had the first telephone line installed in Parliament Building running from the office of Minister of the Interior, S. G. Wilder to the lumber yard. Another set was installed from the Palace to the King's boathouse.

Queen Kapiolani and her nephew Prince David Kawananakoa photographed by Williams.

King Kalakaua and Queen Kapiolani (foreground) in grounds of Iolani Palace.

Bishop Museum

By 1884 the King was being openly criticized in the "opposition" newspapers. S.M. Damon wrote a letter to the Editor of *The Daily Bulletin* (Lorrin Thurston) offering reasons why the King should not be discussed. But Messrs. W.R. Castle, N.B. Emerson and A.S. Hartwell were loudly vocal in defending the "right to discuss the reigning monarch."

The Daily Bulletin continued: "... And wherefore should not we discuss the King? The King is personally and individually responsible for the continuation of the present disreputable and disgraceful condition of affairs. Why should we beat around the bush?"

Hawaii State Archives

Kalakaua sitting on a bench in the Palace grounds. . . next to him is D. Makainai. . . photo taken between 1884-87 by A.A. Montano.

In 1885 the Japanese Government finally decided to allow their people to emigrate to Hawaii; in 1886 a treaty was made between the two nations. Thereafter, the gates opened and several thousand Japanese workers poured into the Islands each successive year. By 1896 the Japanese comprised almost a quarter of the entire population.

Japanese worker in cane field.

Isobel Strong wrote of the ceremony she witnessed, welcoming the first consignment of workers sent from Japan to work on the sugar plantations:

". . . the planters had not been very successful with the people they had tried out on the cane fields. The native Hawaiians were of course, impossible. They laughed and sang, and if the eye of authority left them for a minute, they curled up in the sun and went to sleep. A big consignment of Portuguese from Madeira proved too sturdy and independent to be managed easily. Chinese coolies found housework and storekeeping in the towns so much to their taste that their numbers in the cane fields diminished rapidly and mysteriously. A few black boys from the Caroline Islands and New Guinea simply lay down and died of homesickness. It was the King's idea to import Japanese labourers for the plantations. The first consignment was so large it took more than one ship to bring them. They were housed temporarily in tents on a large field enclosed by a high fence. There were hundreds of them with their wives and children; a gay chattering crowd. . . all in their colourful native dress.

"The King invited us to sit on the platform beside him, while he recieved them officially. Before him, in a dense mass, the men were waiting, and when the King stood up they all threw themselves on their faces at once. It was a startling sight. . . like a sudden wind across a wheat field flattening the grain. Through an interpreter, Kalakaua made a speech of welcome promising them fair wages and good treatment. The response to this was another surprise. The loud shout of another word we had never heard before; Banzai!"

In downtown Honolulu, at four o'clock in the afternoon of Saturday, April 18, 1886, a fire broke out in a Chinese restaurant on Hotel Street. It spread relentlessly throughout the Chinese section of the city until almost 70 acres were reduced to a heap of smouldering ashes. Thousands were left homeless; the damage was estimated at $1.5 million.

Two days later, *The Hawaiian Gazette* reported the King's concern; "... *King Kalakaua did excellent work urging on the willing men and exerting himself to the utmost to stay the raging flames. Again and again did the men under his command strive to stay the flames... and again and again were they driven back."*

Chinatown fire... 1886.

The bungalow; *"Hale Akala"* enclosed by its pink and white lattice. Situated in Iolani Palace grounds, it was the private residence of Kalakaua and the Queen (standing at right).

The Bungalow, *"Hale Akala"* (Pink House) which stood where Iolani Barracks now stands, was a charming, two storeyed, lattice structure which served as a personal residence for the King and Queen when they wished to escape the formality of Palace living. It was demolished in 1919.

Bungalow interior. . . Palace grounds.

A room in the bungalow about 1886.

In the same year, 1886, the King's Jubilee was celebrated with two weeks of festivities in honour of Kalakaua's fiftieth birthday. Among the many parties given there was another *luau* in the Palace grounds for which a *lanai* was constructed covering an area of 250 feet by 35 feet. *The Daily Bulletin* recorded the event: "*. . . the royal table is handsomely laid with trenchers of silver and gold, China ware, silver knives and forks, cut glass in blue, green, and cherry and other rich colours. The table is margined with a stately row of covered calabashes of native woods of most elegant make and finish. Stately silver candelabra are placed at regular intervals. The whole of the table ware is laid in a beautiful expanse of leaves and flowers. . . the menu included pig, raw and cooked fish, beef,* papai *(a kind of crab),* limu, opae, *dried fish,* opelo, awa, *chicken, turkey,* duck, taro, *sweet potatoes, bananas, oranges, champagne, ale and soda water. . .*"

Procession at Kalakaua's Jubilee, November 16th, 1886. King and Queen leading the way. Liliuokalani and her husband John Dominis following.

The procession, Jubilee, 1886.

Hawaii State Archives

Kauai dancers. . . Jubilee celebrations, 1886.

Moanalua dancers at the Jubilee.

At his fiftieth birthday Jubilee, gifts presented to King Kalakaua included several hundred specially made poi bowls.

Hawaii State Archives

Preparations for luau at King's Boathouse. . . Jubilee, November 16th, 1886.

Hawaii State Archives

Hookupu (Gifts) Kalakaua's Jubilee.

"The Spouting Whale". . . Jubilee Procession.

During the year of 1886 King Kalakaua founded Ka Hale Naua (the Temple of Wisdom), a society dedicated to the origin of man and his progress.

In the ceremonies of the society *"The Eternal Virgin"* symbolized *"The Presence of An Immortal Power"* while the hula, in all its esoteric significance, formed an important part of each ritual.

Excerpts from the Hale Naua are reproduced at the end of this book.

Under the patronage of Their Majesties King Kalakaua and Queen Kapiolani, Ka Hale Naua was composed principally of native Hawaiians. Like the ancient Egyptians, the Masonic Order and other fraternal bodies, their proceedings were kept secret from the outside world. Only those considered worthy and acceptable were initiated into the mysteries of the Order. This mode of conducting business was also practised by the Hawaiians of ancient times.

The magazine *Paradise of The Pacific* (founded by the King) reported the following in August 1888: *". . . Having heard much about the society we inquired closely into the matter, and upon investigation we are impelled to acknowledge the good aims of the society, and to give all due credit to the members of the society, and we think that their efforts should receive commendation and encouragement and not ridicule and malice, as has been the case. The greatest possible compliment is paid to the society by that eminent scientific journal 'Engineering' of London, which, in its issue of February 24th, devoted more than a page to one of the papers read by one of the members, the Hon. Antone Rose, entitled 'Diametral Physiography:' "*

Diametral Physiography

"We are indebted for the subjoined diagrams headed "Diametral Physiography" to His Majesty King Kalakaua of the Hawaiian Kingdom (better known by the name of the Sandwich Islands), assisted by his scientific adviser, Mr. J. Degraves, C.E. The diagrams shown are some of a series from which it is intended to construct a model of the world, which model is to be brought before the public at one of the great exhibitions as soon as it is completed. The original idea of His Majesty when starting his researches on exhibiting the shape of the earth's crust looked at from Mr. Green's point of view, and the reader must judge for himself whether Mr. Green's theory is borne out, supposing the heights and soundings given here to be accurate. In any case we are much indebted to His Majesty King Kalakaua and Mr. Degraves for their researches, and look forward to the time when the contemplated models will have arrived at completion."

The constitution of the Hale Naua reads:

"The foundation of the Hale Naua is from the beginning of the world and the revival of the Order was in the month of Welo (September), on the night of Kane, in the reign of His Majesty Kalakaua I., the 825th generation from Lailai, or 24,750 years from the Wohi Kumulipo (the beginning) and Kapomanomano (the producing agent), equivalent to 40,000,000,000,024,750 years from the commencement of the world and 24,750 years from Lailai, the first woman, dating to the date of the present calendar, the 24th of September 1886, A.D."

Article I of the constitution reads:

"The object of this Society is the revival of Ancient Science of Hawaii in combination with the promotion and advancement of Modern Sciences, Art, Literature and Philanthropy."

Edward K. Lilikalani

Antone Rosa

Paradise of the Pacific continued in its praise of the King's Society:

"Ka Hale Naua will send a collection of curiosities to the Melbourne Exhibition. Among the articles there is a feather cape, the art of the manufacture of which has been regarded as a lost art, but has been restored by the exertions of the Society.

"The work assigned to each of the members is entirely local and confined particularly to the Hawaiian Islands. The following is a list of the members composing the scientific branch of the "Hale Naua" of the present year (1888) under the patronage of their Majesties the King and Queen.

"Her Royal Highness Princess Poomaikelani, President; Hon. Antone Rosa, Geology; Hon. J.L. Kaulukou, Dialect and History (Ancient Hawaiian); His Majesty Kalakaua, Biology; Hon. J.A. Cummins, Conchology; Mrs. G. Kahalewai, Botany; Mrs. C.H. Ulukou, Archaeology; Mr. J. Ena, Seismology; Joseph Liwai, Ornithology; Hon. E.K. Lilikalani, Mineralogy; Major J.P. Kahalewai, Meteorology; His Majesty Kalakaua, Geography and Diametral Physiography; Major J.P. Kahalewai, Curator and Museum; Mrs. G. Kahalewai, Secretary."

Another quote from *Engineering* of London, regarding King Kalakaua's work: *"The original idea of His Majesty when starting his researches on this matter was to confute or perhaps confirm the theory broached by Mr. W.L. Green (late Minister of Foreign Affairs to the King and now Prime Minister to His Majesty) in his work entitled 'Vestiges of the Molten Globe,' that the form of the solid crust of the earth is that of a tetahedron. . . the diagrams present sections of the land and sea at certain parallels of latitude affording a new view of our globe which is extremely interesting. Briefly speaking, the idea of His Majesty in the construction of these diagrams was as follows: Here is a theory as to the shape of the molten globe, let us consider the best way of investigating it. The author takes the North Pole as an obtuse solid angle, so that if I take sections along various parallels of latitude normal to the axis of the earth through the poles, the outline of the solid crust thus shown should represent more or less a figure of six sides. . ."*

HS
H3

CONTENTS

Contents of the Constitution of Hale Naua.

Ioane (John) Ukeke, the dandy dance master and leader of King Kalakaua's hula troupe. He was known as: *"The Honolulu Dandy."* Wearing his green silk trousers and purple coat, on *"Steamer Days"* he was often mistaken for the King by visitors. Hula master, dance instructor, banjo strummer, virtuoso on the Jews harp, he moved his hula troupe around Oahu for command performances by the King and to the country luaus of others in the royal circle. After enjoying such glory in the days of Kalakaua, Ioane became nothing more than a blind beggar in the streets of Honolulu when the monarchy was overthrown.

Ioane Ukeke with his dance troupe.

Ioane, the Dandy dance master.

Jennie Wilson (right) was a particular favourite of the King. He called her "Lady Jane."

Under the leadership of King Kalakaua there was a great revival of Hawaiian culture. The King was a patron to all the arts, with a particular interest in music from the ancient chants of his ancestors to the popular waltzes of the day.

Around 1872 Kalakaua met Henry Berger who had been brought from Germany during the reign of Kamehameha V to lead the Royal Hawaiian Band. The two collaborated in the composition of many songs, the best known being Hawaii's national anthem, *"Hawaii Ponoi,"* composed in 1874. The basis for the anthem was actually the Prussian hymn; *"Heil Dir Im Siegerkranz"* which Berger re-arranged while the King wrote the lyrics. As he sought Berger's musical guidance in composing most of his songs, it appears that although Kalakaua was musical, he preferred to write the lyrics. Seven of his songs appear in *"Ka Buke O Na Leo Mele Hawaii"* (Published in 1888) signed with the King's pseudonym, *"Figgs."*

Captain Henry Berger in 1913.

Hawaii State Archives

Kalakaua was an ardent revivalist of the ancient chants and composed several *mele* or chants himself in the 1880's. He formed *hula* clubs, arranged performances of more than 300 ancient *hulas* and created many new ones, blending the old style with the new influences of imported dances. The Hula Ku'i is an example of Spanish dancing merging with traditional Hawaiian movements and performed to the accompaniment of the ukulele, the guitar, the taro patch fiddle (a five stringed instrument) and even the piano. After its first public appearance during the King's Coronation ceremonies in 1883, the Hula Ku'i became the rage.

Nathaniel B. Emerson wrote: *"Even the school children took it up. . . and might frequently be seen innocently footing its measures on the streets. . ."*

Hawaiian music benefited greatly during this renaissance patronized by King Kalakaua, evidenced by the huge output of Hawaiian composition during his reign.

Under the Royal patronage of Kalakaua, the performing arts thrived in the growing town of Honolulu. All kinds of musical activities were organized, including concerts, benefit programs and performances by the Royal Hawaiian Band, while the downtown Opera House staged regular shows from Shakespeare to Italian Opera.

King Kalakaua was a frequent visitor to the down town shop of Augusto Dias who first introduced the King to a small guitar-type instrument brought from the shopkeeper's Portuguese homeland; the ukulele. Dias taught the King how to play it and it became Kalakaua's favourite instrument. He even gave Dias permission to stamp the Royal Crown on every ukulele made in the craftsman's shop.

Kalakaua in Hawaiian Military Uniform.

K alakaua's famed boathouse *"Healani"* was also the scene of the King's Music Club.

Many receptions and *luaus* were held at Healani. While his enemies raved on that he was *". . . reviving vile heathen chants and licentious practices of savage times. . ."* Kalakaua's guests enjoyed performances by the King's group of twelve dancers while Kalakaua himself explained the esoteric meaning of each *hula*.

Contests between Kalakaua's own group of singers and musicians and the groups of his brother Leleiohoku and his sister Liliuokalani often filled the nights with song that echoed across the waters from *"Healani."*

Kalakaua's Boathouse, *"Healani"* jutting out into Honolulu Harbour.

Hawaii State Archives

Kalakaua's six-oared boat crew, the Iolani Boat Club. Some names given: Kalino, Kalua, Kahalewai and John Baker.

Coal Pile.

"Poomaikelani" entered by Iolani Boat Club, Nov. 16, 1885, beat *"Alice M."* Myrtle Boat Club: No. 1, R. Parker, No. 2, J.D. Holt, No. 3, Awana, No. 4, Kaulahao, No. 5, Kaluahine, No. 6, Kaki, stroke, Welau, Coxwain.

On Sunday, May 23rd, 1886, showing his weariness, Prime Minister Gibson wrote in his diary: *". . . This evening with the King . . . Said he wants me five years more . . . and then would let me go."*

The Reciprocity Treaty; neither terminated nor renewed, was kept alive from 1883 to1887 only by Washington's concern over the activities of the British and the Germans in the Pacific.

Enemies of the King as well as competitors of Claus Spreckels and sugar producers on the Mainland all tried to abrogate the treaty long before it expired.

Finally, *Paradise of the Pacific* reported the *"end of the feeling of uncertainty in Hawaii. . .:"*

Prosperity Re-established

"The King's speech, at the opening of the recent extra session of the Legislature, announced that the Treaty of Reciprocity with the United States had been "definitely extended for seven years upon the same terms as those in the original treaty, with the additional clause granting to national vessels of the United States the exclusive privilege of entering Pearl River Harbour, and establishing there a coaling and repair station." He further stated that he regarded it as one of the most important events of his reign. . . the indecision for the past two or three years as to the fate of the treaty has had the effect of checking enterprise. The definite settlement of its renewal will re-establish confidence and warrant the extension of the existing enterprises and the establishment of new ones. Granting to the United States the right to the use of Pearl River Harbour for a coaling and repair station may be followed by the introduction of foreign capital for internal improvements, and naturally an increased attraction to the Islands by all classes of people in recognition of its political and commercial importance. . ."

Princess Liliuokalani wrote the following two entries in her diary:

Sept 25, 1887:
". . . King told me that efforts were being made to cede Pearl Harbour to the U.S. He would resist it. . ."

Sept. 26, 1887:
"Today a day of importance in Hawaiian history. King signed a lease of Pearl River to U.S. for eight years to get Reciprocity Treaty. It should not have been done. . ."

Encouraged by Walter Murray Gibson, King Kalakaua nurtured a vision of an independent Pacific Empire, with Hawaii at its head. In his first step toward this goal he attempted to form an alliance with Samoa in 1886, following reports of rebellion in Samoa against the ruling government of King Malietoa whom many Samoans no longer regarded as King.

For the *"Mission to Samoa"* King Kalakaua appointed a former Cabinet Minister, part-Hawaiian, John E. Bush, as his *"Envoy Extraordinary and High Commissioner to the Sovereign Chiefs and Peoples of Polynesia."*

Envoy Bush received instructions from Gibson to convey King Kalakaua's sympathy *". . . from one Polynesian Monarch to another."* Premier Gibson continued: *". . . if, however, in response to these private and confidential assurances of His Majesty's sympathy, any advances or proposals should come from King Malietoa pointing to such an alliance between Hawaii and Samoa as would give to the former a right to speak authoritatively to Foreign Powers on behalf of the Independence of Samoa. . . you are to express your belief that such an alliance or confederation of the two countries, if made close enough to render them but one state in their relations to foreign powers, will meet with acceptance here. . ."*

Tonga was expected to join in the proposed alliance later.

Meanwhile civil war threatened to erupt in Samoa as two rival chiefs claimed the title of King.

John E. Bush

Into these troubled Samoan waters sailed Envoy Extraordinary Bush, accompanied by his family, a secretary, Henry Poor, and Joe Strong (husband of Isobel), an artist, on December 23rd, 1886. Bush was to propose Samoa's confederation with Hawaii.

On January 7th, 1887 King Malietoa, from his shaky throne, warmly received the visitors from Hawaii. Celebrations went on all night. Finally, after consultations with his advisers, Malietoa signed an agreement with Bush on February 17th "*. . . to enter into the installation of confederation. . .*"

At King Kalakaua's request Bush then conferred on Malietoa the Grand Cross of The Order of The Star of Oceania: *"as having been established to distinguish the Kings and Nobles of Polynesia and those who help to bring prosperity and progress to the people of Polynesia."*

King Malietoa replied in part: *". . . I give full praise to King Kalakaua for his esteemed demonstration of concern. It is true that the Hawaiian and Samoan people are related kinfolk. . ."*

Kalakaua's Naval ship, "Kaimiloa"; Honolulu Harbour, circa 1885.

Always a lover of ships, Kalakaua inaugurated his Hawaiian Navy with the purchase of one ship; a decrepit copra trader of 171 tons sent to Honolulu for repairs.

Formerly the British steamer *Explorer*, she was bought by the Hawaiian Government for $20,000, refitted and armed with brass cannon and gatling guns *"for the naval service of the Kingdom,"* and finally re-named *Kaimiloa* (The Far Seeker).

The original commission of *Kaimiloa* as a man-o-war was changed to *"naval training ship."* In April 1887, she was placed under the command of a Briton, Captain George E. Gresley Jackson, the Principal of the Reformatory School in Honolulu. Two dozen boys from Jackson's school were taken as trainee seamen on the *Kaimiloa*. The remainder of the crew of sixty-three consisted of three other officers beside Capt. Jackson; Lieutenant Samuel Ikuwa Maikai, Assistant Lieutenant C.H. Kaulukou, Lieutenant of the Soldiers Frank Jerome Waiau, marines from the King's Guard and other experienced sailors.

Kalakaua on board *"Kaimiloa"*. . . to the right his equerry, Antone Rosa. Most of the seamen were boys from the Reform School.

Premier Gibson also sent Joseph S. Webb as an official passenger *". . . to ascertain the true condition of affairs in Samoa."* After many delays in Honolulu, including a riot on board before she even left the wharf, the *Kaimiloa* proudly set sail for Samoa on the morning of May 18th, 1887.

Awaiting the arrival in Samoa of Kalakaua's ship, the Hawaiian Embassy under John Bush was disappointed to discover that the ship was not a man-o-war after all, but a naval training vessel. Conditions in Samoa were becoming so tense that the Hawaiians felt it might be necessary to fire a shot or two.

Meanwhile the *Kaimiloa's* main purpose was to ferry Bush and party among the Island Groups considered for the Federation. It was thought that a Hawaiian Navy man-o-war might make a good impression on the Island people of that area.

Joseph Webb's first letter back to Gibson after *Kaimiloa's* arrival on June 15th reported complications: "*. . . Things have been worse than I deemed possible. On hearing, however, that I was on board the* Kaimiloa, *Mr. Bush made a desperate effort, and after passing through that sort of 'bad time' which follows indulgence, has for a fortnight been very temperate and more discreet in his personal conduct. If letters do not come to hand with instructions from Your Excellency, I shall use my best endeavours to get him off to Tonga promptly. He cannot recover himself here. The majority of the Chiefs are sober men and feel very much that the Hawaiian Chief on whom they relied should not disgrace himself.*

"*Malietoa, a very temperate and religious man, sent for him twice to expostulate with him, and on one occasion, kept him at Afenga several days in order that he might get straight. As to that part of the foreign population who ought to be the best friends of the Hawaiian Embassy, I am told that a large majority keep aloof, and all pray to see a change. If I gave Your Excellency the details that have come to my knowledge you would be unexpressibly astonished and shocked and have no wonder at the general sentiment prevailing here. . .*"

Malietoa's Assistant Secretary of State also wrote to Premier Gibson of Envoy Bush's *"disreputable conduct"*: "*. . . He is the most dissipated man who has held a high position at this place for many years. His associates here are mostly the lowest kind of half-castes and whites. . .*"

Meanwhile, unknown to both complainants, Bush had already been recalled to Hawaii, following a political upheaval there in late June. But the letter of instruction to return was delayed on a slow mail boat. So Bush continued touring the Islands, displaying the Hawaiian flag on the *Kaimiloa*.

But news of the Hawaiian visit to Samoa had reached Prince Bismarck in Germany by this time, and his annoyance was great. He ordered a corvette, the *Adler,* to carefully watch the Hawaiian ship's course in Samoan waters.

Hawaii State Archives

Kaimiloa and *Adler* salute the Samoan flag in Samoa.

Reports of the Samoan-Hawaiian Confederation agreement now angered the governments of three nations with interests in Samoa: Great Britain, the United States and Germany. Secretary Henry Poor who had arrived in Samoa months before with Envoy Bush and family, wrote to Hawaii's Minister of Foreign Affairs, Godfrey Brown, on July 7th, regarding the sad decline of the *Kaimiloa's* prestige:

". . . the first appearance of the Kaimiloa *in Apia produced a most favourable impression among foreigners and natives alike. Her cadet band also became popular. . . and their concerts were an appreciated treat to the Apians. But things soon changed, and the* Kaimiloa *finally became a disgrace to her flag. The captain was taken sick. . . and then all discipline was at an end. The native officers were utterly incompetent . . . and excepting Lieutenant Waiau, they conducted themselves in the most scandalous manner ashore, entirely neglecting their duties on shipboard. There was a state of continuous insubordination on the ship, and utter disregard of all order and discipline. With a few exceptions, the marines and white sailors behaved badly. . . the marines continually breaking liberty by swimming ashore and disturbing the town with their drunken conduct.*

I must say a word in praise of the Reform School Boys. . . . It was a matter of surprise to me to observe how well they behaved on shore and aboard. . . and how well they performed their duties; a fact which was commented on favourably in Apia. Had the Kaimiloa *been organized differently, she might have been creditable as a training ship. . . and been a success, instead of the wretched and disgraceful failure she has proved."*

During August the disgraced *Kaimiloa* left Apia to limp back to Honolulu. . .

Envoy Bush and his family decided to stay longer in Apia and eventually returned to Honolulu in November.

The German Government issued a terse statement in August: *". . . In case Hawaii, whose King acts according to financial principles which it is not desirable to extend to Samoa, should try to interfere in favour of Malietoa, the King of the Sandwich Islands would thereby enter into a state of war with us. . ."*

The Germans then declared war on King Malietoa *"personally."* Malietoa, fearing loss of life amongst his people, surrendered to the Germans, then disappeared into exile. His rival Tamasese was then proclaimed King.

King Kalakaua's dreams of Empire died as the *Kaimiloa* sailed sadly back into Honolulu Harbour on September 23rd, 1887.

The U.S. Secretary of State commented: *"The proximate cause of Malietoa's misfortunes was the ill-starred and mischievous mission of Mr. Bush from the King of Hawaii."*

Later, Kalakaua defended his actions in Samoa in a letter to the Hawaiian Consul in San Francisco, D. McKinley: *". . . Of course I did send Bush. . . but it was from a repeated call from Samoa. . . as well as the other South Sea Islands. . . a call of Confederation or solidarity of the Polynesian race. Our Mission was simply a mission of Phylanthropy more than anything, but the arrogance of the Germans prevented our good intentions and we had to withdraw the Mission. . ."*

King Malietoa on board H.M.S. *Kaimiloa*. Left to Right: Moses Mahelona, Jerome Feary, Sam Maikai, King Malietoa, John Bush, Henry Poor.

Kaimiloa's band in background. Left to right: Hoa C. Ulukou and Sam Maikai, Hawaiian Naval Officers; J. S. Webb, King Kalakaua's Representative; Mataafa, Chief of Atua; John E. Bush, Cabinet Minister; Henry F. Poor, Secretary of the Legation; Jerome Feary, Officer on *Kaimiloa; ?* officer of German warship *Adler.*

In the 1880's both Kalakaua and Gibson were heavily in debt to Claus Spreckels, *"The Sugar King."*

It seemed that the government and practically the entire Kingdom of Hawaii was in Spreckels' hands. He could do as he wished, as he held more than half the national debt. In the Legislature of 1882 a bill was passed to mint and circulate silver coins bearing the head of Kalakaua. Claus Spreckels personally made a profit of $150,000 out of this coinage transaction.

By the middle of 1886 much tension had developed around the working triumvirate of Kalakaua, Gibson and Spreckels. Everywhere people were calling Spreckels *"The King,"* much to the annoyance of the real Monarch.

Kalakaua and Gibson wracked their brains for ways to become financially free of Mr. Spreckels, eventually arranging to borrow two million dollars from the British, more than enough to pay Spreckels back in full.

Hawaii State Archives

Financier Claus Spreckels.

Royal luau at King's Boathouse in honour of Mr. and Mrs. Hoffnung of London.

Worried about his enormous financial stake in Hawaii, Claus Spreckels himself was already alarmed at the King's *"extravagance. . . and the irresponsibliity of Gibson and his Cabinet. . ."*

Meanwhile Gibson wrote in his diary on March 25th: *". . . Spreckels wants our credit with Hoffnung in London to be injured. Wants to prevent our chances of an English loan. . ."*

Then on June 23rd another entry read: *"We approach a Ministerial crisis. . ."*

June 24th: *"Mr. Spreckels at my house. His earnest assurances. . . but he does not always keep his word. But I doubt not his friendly feeling to me . . . The King said this evening that Ministry should resign at the close of session. . ."*

June 26th: *"The King tells Spreckels that he will dismiss the Ministry and have a new Cabinet. . . Creighton, Foreign Affairs, Iaukea, Interior. . . Kanoa, Finance. . . Dare, Atty. Gen. . . ."*

During the legislative session of August 12th Rep. Dickey asked Gibson why he had imported two Ministers, Dare and Creighton from California. . . if he *"had such love for the Hawaiians. . . ,"* reported *The Gazette.*

Gibson replied that the choice had been *"His Majesty's. . ."* A fuming Lorrin Thurston stood up and shouted: *"His Majesty Kalakaua or His Majesty Spreckels?"*

The Saturday Press commented on the situation: *". . . the Government for the last two years has been run in the interests of Mr. Spreckels and today his dictation of the national policy is still submitted to. . ."*

But *The Pacific Commercial Advertiser* defended the financier: *". . . he is endeavouring with all his energies to see us safe over an inevitable depression. . ."*

By this time the friendship between the sugar magnate and the King had deteriorated to the point where a disgusted Spreckels returned the Royal decorations Kalakaua had conferred on him during their *"card playing days."*

After arriving back in San Francisco, Spreckels criticized Kalakaua openly saying he was *". . . a man who could not be reached by calm reason. . . His gin drinking friends fill his head with wild schemes for spending money until Kalakaua has become crazy upon the subject of loans."*

After Spreckels' departure for the mainland, the ever-loyal Gibson wrote: *". . . It is the general belief in Honolulu that the Government is now stronger than ever. But my paper is silent. It is proper for the victors to be silent and thankful and let the losers rail if they like. Our enemies give me credit for having subdued Spreckels. . . and checkmated their plans. This is only partly true. The chief credit should go to the firmness of the King. . ."*

The King at the front entrance to Iolani Palace.

During a visit to the Palace in 1887 Isobel Strong asked the King, with whom she was on friendly terms: *". . . I would like to know why the Missionary Party is making so much trouble for your Majesty?"*

"It is not me, personally, at all. . ." he explained. *"What they want is my country. They are hoping to annex Hawaii to the United States. It has been a steady fight ever since I came to the throne. . ."*

"I was appalled," Strong remembered. *"Take the Islands away from you? Surely they couldn't do that!"*

"Not while I live," said the King.

Kalakaua in the uniform of a Scottish Rite Mason. Lodge Le Progres de L'Oceanie No. 124, A.and A.S.R. Honolulu A.I.

Bishop Museum

Celebration at Pavilion, Hulihee Palace, Kailua, Kona honoring King Kalakaua. (King at railing.)

Hawaii State Archives

Hawaiian opera house on King Street - 1880's.

The so-called *"Bayonet Constitution"* of 1887 greatly curtailed the authority and prestige of King Kalakaua. Under the new law, Cabinet Ministers could not be dismissed by the King unless the vote of the Legislature was in accord; and Kalakaua could make no official act without the approval of the Cabinet.

A committee of thirteen non-Hawaiians presented the new resolutions to the King and Dr. Nathaniel B. Emerson seconded the motion.

The Hon. Paul Isenberg called for *"moderation"* and *"fair play"* but the keystone had already been laid for complete seizure of the Islands, five and a half years later.

Early in the year of 1887 a secret political organization, The Hawaiian League, was formed which aimed to reform the government by devising a *"more liberal constitution."*

Its members were foreigners or Hawaiian citizens (born in Hawaii or naturalized), but not one native Hawaiian belonged to the League.

Gibson was accused of *"stirring up racial antagonism"* with his *"Hawaii for the Hawaiians"* slogan. He seemed dedicated to arousing hatred against non-Hawaiians who comprised most of the businessmen of Hawaii. And now that the idea for a Polynesian Empire, fostered by himself and the King, had exploded in their faces, Gibson's enemies were jubilant.

Gibson wrote a troubled comment in his diary on June 27th, 1887. regarding *". . . Assurances of a widespread and dangerous organization to subvert the government. . ."*

The Hawaiian League feared the rise of Hawaiian patriotism. Of its two factions, one wanted a *"Monarchy reform"* to take away Kalakaua's power. The other was dedicated to a clearcut *"annexation to the United States."* Secretly, the three companies of Hawaiian Rifles which had always received government support, now became the League's *"military arm."*

Under mounting pressure in Honolulu, Gibson and the entire Ministry resigned on Tuesday, June 28th, 1888. He appeared to accept his fate as he wrote: *". . . meeting of Ministers at 10 a.m. . . . resigned our offices. Hope that our resignations will quiet the public's feeling. . ."* Then on June 29th he added: *". . . a somewhat easier feeling since announcement of resignation of Ministers. The King now alarmed. . . will accept the extreme radicals. Probable Ministry. . . W.L. Green, Godfrey Brown, J.O. Carter and Sanford B. Dole. . ."*

Kalakaua and Gibson believed that the swift removal of the hated Prime Minister from office would be enough to quieten the loud clamour for reform. But they were wrong as the turbulent events of the following days were to show.

On June 30th a great mass meeting was called at the Armory of the Honolulu Rifles, on the corner of Beretania and Punchbowl streets. By two o'clock in the afternoon, the building was overflowing with an excited crowd eager to hear the outpourings of the Hawaiian League and its *"Committee of Thirteen"* who by now appeared to be drunk with power.

Lorrin Thurston, dressed in the uniform of the all-*haole* Honolulu Rifles, took the speaker's stand first. His speech was more dramatic than ever as he waved his arms and shouted his demand for the *"overthrow of the King and his government!"* Thurston was followed to the speaker's stand by ardent followers, each voicing support of the King's overthrow. German sugar planter Paul Isenberg, desperately tried to inject some common sense into the hysterical meeting: *"I'll approve of a new constitution,"* he said, *"but only if passed by the Legislature."*

Bishop Museum

Walter Murray Gibson

He was booed by the crowd.

Col. V.V. Ashford, resplendent in his uniform of the Commander of the Honolulu Rifles, moved to the speaker's stand while his militia marched noisily into the building in a display of their might. *"If we have to fight. . . by the name of heaven we will!"* Ashford shrieked to the now frenzied spectators.

An alarmed British Commissioner noted that: *". . . both parties were armed and ready for a struggle. The Palace was strongly fortified. . . could not have been taken without great loss of life. Had therefore His Majesty not placed himself in our hands unreservedly, bloodshed must have ensued. . . and as the demands made (by the Mass Meeting) were in our opinion not un-reasonable, we had no hesitation in advising him to comply with them. . ."*

Meanwhile an ashen faced Gibson was pacing the floor at his home Hal-aaniani on King Street, where he was detained under armed guard as the Committee of Thirteen, the sterling body of the Hawaiian League, feared that he and the King might get their heads together and plan a *"coup d'etat."*

A weary King Kalakaua yielded to the demands of the *"Reformers"* which he recorded as follows: *". . . the formal resignation of the Ministry. . . on the 28th of June. . . Hon. W.L. Green has been requested to form a new government. Mr. Walter M. Gibson has severed all his connections with the Hawaiian Government by resignation. Mr. Junius Kaae, Registrar of Convey-ances resigned his office. . . ."*

The new Reform Cabinet was sworn in immediately: William Lowthian Green, Minister of Finance; Godfrey Brown, Minister of Foreign Affairs; Lorrin Thurston, Minister of the Interior; Clarence Ashford, Attorney Gene-ral. . .

All were British except Thurston.

Gibson wrote on June 30th of: *". . . threats of violence. . . . The Rifles at the Govt. Building. . . . I address a note to Lieut. Col. Ashford asking pro-tection of Rifles. He ordered a detachment under Capt. Fisher to guard my residence. I go to Govt. Building to be protected there. Removal of Guard. . . return to my house. Rumours of armed mob. . . purpose to lynch me. Col. Ashford informs me that I will be shot down if I attempt to leave my house. The mob around my house. . . an anxious night. Faithful guard of Dan Lyons (Editor of the* Elele*)."*

By July 1st conditions were worse as Gibson shakily reported: *". . . Fred (son-in-law Hayselden) returned from beach this morning. Whilst we were talking together in the parlour about ten a.m., Col. Ashford entered and ordered us peremptorily to put on our hats and go with him. A detach-ment of Rifles in the yard marched us off to the Pacific Navigation Co. warehouse. . . an evident purpose to hang us. . . . Talula,"*(Gibson's daughter) *"arrived. . . pushed her way through the crowd. The Committee of Thirteen released us. We are marched back to the house. Soon after arrested on a charge of embezzlement. Marched to Police Station. Allowed to return to house and remain there under guard. . ."*

Fred W. Hayselden

On that dark day for Gibson and Hayselden the ropes were already flung over high beams in the warehouse, the nooses already tightened around their necks by the men of the Honolulu Rifles when Talula hysterically fought her way through the jeering crowd, followed by a puffing, angry British Consul, James Wodehouse, who roared that Gibson was a *"British subject!"* Their arrival stopped the hanging.

But now the exhausted Gibson and Fred were marched to Oahu Prison where they were detained in a cramped, dirty cell on charges of *"embezzlement of public funds."* Gibson's home was ransacked as the accusers searched for evidence that the Gibson family had taken *"Crown and State money for their own use. . ."*

Finally the case of Hawaii vs. Gibson and Hayselden was heard before the new *"Judge,"*; Attorney General C.W. Ashford, brother of Col. V. Ashford who had earlier arranged the aborted lynching of the two prisoners.

No substantive evidence of embezzlement was ever found, but still *"Judge"* Ashford rendered his verdict in insulting terms to the gaunt, white haired Gibson: His life would be spared if he left Honolulu. Fred Hayselden was also freed.

Several months later, *The San Francisco Examiner* of December 15th reported that *"Gibson was writing a book on Hawaiian history. . . including the revolution of 1887. . . . He intends dropping a large sized bombshell into the camp of his enemies. . ."*

On July 12th a saddened Walter Murray Gibson sailed from Honolulu bound for San Francisco on an old sugar boat named the *J.D. Spreckels* after one of Claus Spreckels' sons.

By the end of 1887 Gibson observed from San Francisco that, despite his reduced power, King Kalakaua was making skillful use of vetoes. He also took advantage of dissension among the reformers.

In an interview with the *San Francisco Call* on December 29th Gibson expressed his surprise at "*. . . the boldness of Kalakaua's vetoes. . . it shows that there is now a sustaining power behind him. . .*"

And further according to the *Call*, Gibson hinted that he "*. . . would soon return to Hawaii . . . to take hold of the reins again. . .*" But Walter Murray Gibson died suddenly after catching cold during a photography session on January 21st, 1888. The immediate cause of death was consumption aggravated by pneumonia and pleurisy combined.

On January 23rd, the *Daily Alta of California* wrote that "*. . . Gibson's last intelligible word was 'Hawaii'* " The ex-Prime Minister's body was embalmed and shipped back to Honolulu for burial in a box covered with the Hawaiian flag.

King Kalakaua was noticeably absent from Gibson's funeral although many of his representatives were among the mourners.

Iolani Palace

Always termed a *"...bitter, unscrupulous man"* by Premier Gibson, Lorrin Thurston was the first to form the idea of the Hawaiian League early in 1887, following a discussion with a Honolulu physican, Dr. S.G. Tucker, *"To reform the Government and limit the powers of the King...so that he would reign...but not rule."*

Records of the League indicate those who were quick to join Thurston: W.A. Kinney (Thurston's partner in a law firm), W.R. Castle, P.C. Jones, C.W. Ashford, Dr. G.H. Martin, W.E. Rowell, Sanford B. Dole, Major H. Benson, A.T. Atkinson, Dr. Nathaniel B. Emerson, C. Furneaux and H. Riemenschneider.

The names of the *"Committee of Thirteen"* were kept secret, but it was widely believed that most of the early members of the League comprised the Thirteen.

In the winter of 1886/87 ugly rumours rang through Honolulu, connecting the King with bribery which involved the granting of an opium license.

One report said that Junius Kaae (the King's Registrar of Conveyances) had talked Tong Kee, a Chinese rice farmer usually known as Aki, into giving a present of $71,000 to King Kalakaua in return for an opium license.

Patiently Aki waited to receive his license which had been authorized by the Legislature of 1886.

But, in the meantime, another Chinese, Chun Lung, paid $80,000...and the Cabinet granted the coveted opium license to him instead.

The scandal rocked Honolulu in late May 1887, at a time when Kalakaua and his Prime Minister Gibson were still mopping up after their disastrous *Kaimiloa* mission...and their wrecked plans for the *"Primacy of The Pacific"* dream.

Just when it seemed that Aki himself was about to come forward and make a statement (which would have cleared the King's name)...he died under mysterious circumstances. It was widely believed that he was poisoned.

A worried Kalakaua was at the time reportedly a quarter of a million dollars in debt.

Curtis P. Iaukea

Gibson wrote of the Aki case in his diary on April 29th, 1887: "*. . . the King returned late yesterday evening from Waimanalo. Saw His Majesty this morning. . . in good spirits. Referred to opium money. . . said Kaae had it in his possession. . . with letters from T. Aki making it an absolute gift to His Majesty. . .*"

The records of the Cabinet Council of July 11, 1887 show that the liquidating of the King's present liabilities "*was being considered. . . including $71,000 due the estate of Aki. The King's debts amounting in all to about $250,000. . . .*"

Kalakaua's disastrous financial affairs were then placed in the hands of trustees.

The Aki Case was finally heard by Judge Edward Preston.

While *The Advertiser* reported the progress of the hearing: "*The defendant, C.P. Iaukea, then His Majesty's Chamberlain and Private Secretary, endeavoured to raise a sufficient sum by mortgage of His Majesty's private property to satisfy the claim or a part of it, applied to the defendant Damon who declined. . . .and the loan was not effected. Mr. Thurston testified that the sole object of the Cabinet was to settle this claim. . . and that they were not interested in obtaining payment of the debts or claims of other creditors, but upon receiving a statement of the amount of the King's debts from Mr. Iaukea, they were so astonished at the amount that they thought it would not be right to pay this claim in preference to the others. . . and ultimately advised His Majesty to make an assignment in trust for the Payment of all claims pro rata, and the trust deed before the Court after negotiations with some of the principal creditors as to who should be the trustees and as to the payment of this claim was executed, Mr. Castle assenting to the arrangement on behalf of Aki. . .*

"*Mr. Castle testifies that at or about the time the deed was executed, His Majesty sent for him and that he met His Majesty at the Bungalow in the Palace grounds when His Majesty admitted he had received the money. . . and was alone responsible for it.*"

Judge Preston finally reached his decision on September 21, 1888, declaring "*that the complainants' claim against the defendants for the sum of $71,000 is established as just and correct within the meaning of the deed of trust in the bill mentioned and that the complainants are entitled to be paid pro rata with other approved claims . . . and order the defendants to pay the same accordingly out of the moneys which may have come to their hands under the trust of the said deed. . . .*"

Isobel Strong recalled the reunion of King Kalakaua and Queen Emma whom he defeated in the Royal Election of 1874. Their meeting took place on board the U.S.S. *Adams* which was in the port of Honolulu in July 1888:

"*. . . We heard excited whispers: 'Queen Emma is here. . . and Kalakaua is coming! How will they meet?'*

"*Looking up at the quarterdeck, we saw a black robed figure in a group of officers that stood about the throne prepared for her rival. . .*

"*Guests came pouring over the side, and then exactly on time (for the King was always punctual) the ship shook with the boom of cannon that announced his arrival. Twenty four guns, when you are on the ship that is firing them, make a tremendous din. As His Majesty stepped on the deck, the ship's band burst into "Hawaii Ponoi." Kalakaua and his handsome equerries, Capt. Haley, the Hawaiian Major and several others, all in flattering uniforms, made a fine looking group. We, the assembled guests, opened a lane to the companionway. . . the men bending from the waist. . . the women sinking in deep curtsies as the King walked slowly along, bowing graciously to right and left, his companions gazing straight ahead haughtily ignoring our presence.*

"*Breathlessly, the crowd below watched His Majesty mount the companionway; when he reached the quarter-deck, he was greeted by the Captain who motioned towards the Throne. . . where Queen Emma stood.*

"*Kalakaua stepped forward; a gallant figure in white and gold, bowed low to the lady in black, and offered her his hand, which she took and was about to kiss. With a quick, dextrous movement he gave her a little whirl and a push that seated her on the throne.*

"*Queen Emma's surprised face was almost comic when the King bowed again before her. Then she smiled sweetly, he leaned over and they talked together with such evident friendliness that we all felt like applauding.*

"*After that the two were friends. . . and I often saw Queen Emma at the King's formal parties. . .*"

Kapiolani and Liliuokalani attending Queen Victoria's Jubilee in London, 1887.

Queen Kapiolani photographed in London, 1887 by Walery of Regent Street, wearing dress made in Japan.

Queen Kapiolani and Princess Liliuokalani in London, 1887.

Hawaii State Archives

J.M. Kapena - Twice Minister of Finance
during Kalakaua's reign.

Hawaii State Archives

Lorrin A. Thurston Minister of Interior
in 1887, aged 29.

Charles Reed Bishop wrote to Rudolph W. Meyer on January 7, 1887: "... *It is true that Kalakaua is not to be entrusted with much power; but so long as he is King he is entitled to respectful treatment, on account of his office if for no other reason, and all such remarks as you mention, either verbal or written are wrong and will do harm. There is occasion for great patience and forbearance all round, so that affairs may be settled and work smoothly...*"

And further on June 27, 1887: "... *Whichever way I turn affairs look discouraging to me. Demoralization is going on among the Hawaiians, and they do not realise their shame and danger. How much they need a good leader of their own race, a man of talents, character and eloquence.*"

Again Charles Reed Bishop wrote on January 2, 1888: "... *To adapt a Constitution to such a mixed population, of such a range of intelligence, to such a King and such a condition of affairs as existed in June last, required more wisdom than I profess I have. The central idea was to curtail the power of the King and make the Ministers responsible; to place the authority and responsibility in the same hands, and that should be kept in mind constantly. The King cannot be reached by law, but the Ministers can be...*"

Towards the end of Kalakaua's reign the bitter feeling between pro-Hawaiian and opposing *"Missionary"* groups had developed into an active political movement.

Ralph Kuykendall observed in his book *The Hawaiian Kingdom:* *"In the succeeding period we observe what was apparently a deliberate effort to separate natives and foreigners and foment race hatred. The cry was raised, 'Hawaii for Hawaiians,' and this slogan was used to promote the political interests of various persons. That a feeling of racial antagonism existed is clearly apparent. That this feeling intensified in the reign of Kalakaua is equally clear. To apportion the blame for its existence and intensification is not easy."*

The Constitution of 1887 which stripped the King of most of his power and engendered increasing trouble in the ranks of the haole Reform Party, met with a rising tide of opposition which finally erupted in the rebellion of 1889 led by Robert W. Wilcox.

In her book *Hawaii's Story by Hawaii's Queen* Liliuokalani wrote of her indignation and astonishment one day during the Legislative Session of 1888 when James Dowsett Jr., the eighteen-year-old spokesman for the Missionary Party, came to her house at Muulaulani, Palama, to inquire whether she would accept the throne should her brother be dethroned. Hers was a final *"no."*

She then asked the intention of the Missionary Party. . . what they proposed to do to her brother in order to dethrone him. Were they going to murder him? Young Dowsett answered that he knew nothing more about it, then he left.

Within days Liliuokalani had a similar call from W.R. Castle who added the assurance that she would be supported by the Missionary Party should she replace Kalakaua on the throne. Liliuokalani also asked of Castle whether the Missionary Party meant harm to the King's person. He denied any intent but said that Kalakaua must retire and Liliuokalani should resume his position as reigning sovereign.

To Mr. Castle Liliuokalani firmly stated that she would have nothing to do with this matter. She wrote further; *"Seeing that I firmly declined the proposal, Mr. Castle retired and as that was the last I heard about it, I infer that having made their plots, they lacked the courage or the heart to put their plans into execution. . ."*

British Commissioner James H. Wodehouse wrote the following confidential despatch to the Foreign Office on July 28th, 1888: *". . . Princess Liliuokalani, the King's sister and Heiress Apparent to the Throne, is I fancy, cherishing hopes of the King's abdication . . . and her views are probably shared by Mr. A. S. Cleghorn whose daughter (Kaiulani) would then be next in succession. It is fair to say that both the King's sister and Mr. Cleghorn have grounds for their dislike of the King, inasmuch as his pet project was to substitute his nephew Prince David (Kawananakoa) as his successor in the place of his sister, and so utterly destroy the chances of Mr. Cleghorn's daughter, the Princess Kaiulani."*

King Kalakaua and Military Staff. Left to right rear: Col. James H. Boyd, Col. Curtis P. Iaukea, Major Edward Purvis, Col. George H. Macfarlane, Captain A. B. Hayley, Major J. D. Holt, Major Antone Rosa. Front Row: Col. Charles H. Judd, Kalakaua and Gov. J. O. Dominis.

In the Legislative sessions of 1887 and 1888 the Reform Party set out religiously to remove every vestige of King Kalakaua's influence from the government of Hawaii. Sadly the King saw them vote down all his favourite projects: the native Hawaiian Board of Health was abolished, so was the Board of Genealogists, the Hawaiian Navy was finished and control of the armed forces was taken from the King and given to Godfrey Brown, the Reformers' Minister of Foreign Affairs. As a final blow the three Hawaiian boys whose education Kalakaua was sponsoring in Europe were called abruptly home.

Robert Wilcox, one of the three summoned home by the Reform Party was cruelly scorned back in Hawaii. Jobless and frustrated, he rebelled.

By June 1889 in a Palama house lent to him by Liliuokalani, Wilcox was holding secret meetings with a small group of restless Hawaiians and foreigners who were *"fed up"* with the Reform Party and all it stood for.

Towards the end of July, Wilcox had inspired eighty men, all of whom he dressed in red Garibaldi shirts while he wore his Italian officer's uniform.

At three o'clock in the morning of July 30 Wilcox led his followers in a march to Iolani Palace, bearing a new constitution for King Kalakaua to sign. But Kalakaua was not at home. He was spending the night at his wife's residence, but on hearing of the *"night callers"* he went to his boathouse where he remained secluded, ignoring pleas from Wilcox to return to the Palace and sign the document. Meanwhile Wilcox's revolutionaries were barred from entering the Palace, so they spent the last few hours of darkness in the Palace grounds and in the Government office buildings across King Street.

By mid-morning of the next day, July 31, the first shot was fired. Then loud volleys from the Honolulu Rifles forced Wilcox and friends into the Bungalow in the Palace grounds. Dynamite was thrown onto the roof tearing it to pieces with a deafening blast. Reluctantly one of Wilcox's gallant men came out through the smoke, waving a small ragged white flag tied to a stick. His colleagues followed and the uprising was quelled. Seven of Wilcox's men were killed, twelve wounded.

Later, during his *"trial for treason,"* Robert Wilcox said he wanted the King to sign a *"new constitution which would restore the old prerogatives of the King and the people. . . ."* Claiming that he had Kalakaua's sanction for his acts, Wilcox was acquitted by a native jury.

Damage to the bungalow's interior. Photo taken after the Wilcox Revolution of 1889.

The revolutionary Robert Wilcox.

Col. Volney V. Ashford, a Canadian arrived
in Hawaii early in 1885 and joined his
younger brother Clarence in a law firm.

Hawaii State Archives

Col. Clarence W. Ashford in the uniform of the Honolulu Rifles, 1888.

Hawaii State Archives

The King and friends in Kona.

Kapiolani, Kalakaua, John Cummins and party at Cook's Monument, Kaawaloa, Waimea, Hawaii in 1888.

Kalakaua and party at the home of Thomas E. Evans, Lahaina, October 11 - 18th 1889. The King and Princess Poomaikelani entertained Prince and Princess Henri de Bourbon and members of the Evans family.

The Census of 1890

The report of the General Superintendent of the Census; C.T. Rodgers showed a total population of 89,990 in the Hawaiians Islands in the year 1890.

Native Hawaiians. . . 34,436

Half castes. . . 6186

Hawaiian-born foreigners. . . 7495

Americans. . . 1928

British. . . 1344

Germans. . . 1034

French. . . 70

Portuguese. . . 8602

Norwegians. . . 227

Chinese. . . 15,301

Japanese. . . 12,360

Polynesians. . . 588

Other nationalities. . . 419

Total. 89,990

Luau given by Henry Poor at his Waikiki home for the King and the Stevenson family in 1889. Kalakaua is seated at the head of the table with his sister Liliuokalani at his right and R. L. Stevenson beside her. On the King's left is Mrs. Thomas Stevenson, the writer's mother. On the left side front is Joe Strong, the artist and across from him, facing the camera is his wife Isobel Strong.

Scottish writer Robert Louis Stevenson, visiting Honolulu in 1889, wrote to his friends of King Kalakaua: *"He is a gentleman of courtly order and much tinctured with letters. . ."*

Then to his friend Charles Baxter, February 8th 1889:

"His Majesty is a very fine intelligent fellow. But, oh, Charles! What a crop for the drink! He carries it too—like a mountain with a sparrow on its shoulders. . .

"Kalakaua is a terrible companion; a bottle of fizz is like a glass of sherry to him; he thinks nothing of five or six in an afternoon as a whet for dinner. You should see a photograph of us after an afternoon with his Hawaiian Majesty. My what a crew!"

By 1890, King Kalakaua was aided by the formation of a society of native Hawaiians called Hui Kalaiaina, a name which translated into the English language meant *"The Hawaiian Political Association."* It was first organized at a well-attended rally on the night of November 22, 1888 when John E. Bush was elected President. Robert W. Wilcox was also an ardent member. The society's purpose was to restore the Constitution of 1864 (Wilcox's cry) which would *"guarantee supremacy of the King. . ."*

Through the efforts of Hui Kalaiaina the King's Party did grow stronger, while the Reform Party, now weakened by quarrels and dissension among its members, did not have a majority in the Legislature of 1890. Clarence Ashford squabbled with most of his colleagues while Lorrin Thurston was quite paranoid by this time sniffing out *"a traitor in their midst."* Eventually the Reform Party dissolved itself on June 13th. Thurston and Ashford both resigned followed by two other Cabinet members. When the Reform Cabinet fell from power, it took with it another old adversary of the King; the four companies of the Honolulu Rifles were dissolved by the Legislature.

King Kalakaua with Col. C.H. Judd (left) and Col. G.W. Macfarlane (right).

Merchant Street looking towards Waikiki from Nuuanu Avenue. . . August 1890.

On June 17 a happier Kalakaua announced a new Ministry headed by a friend, the genial John A. Cummins. But Wilcox and Bush were not yet satisfied. Still brandishing the *"Constitution of 1864,"* they wanted to see the King restored to full power as in the days of old. Arguments followed on the floor of the Assembly, along with troubled mass meetings throughout Honolulu.

In mid-August, 1890, forty-three native Hawaiians marched to Iolani Palace, accompanied by the Royal Hawaiian Band playing full blast. They presented a petition to the King to rewrite the Constitution, *"the same as in 1864. . ."* But the Constitution was never revised under Kalakaua.

At the closing of the Legislative session on November 14, 1890, many were shocked at Kalakaua's appearance of ill health. Soon after, it was announced that the King would take a few months vacation in the cooler climate of San Francisco. The flagship *Charleston* was offered for the King's voyage by a close friend of Kalakaua; Rear-Admiral George Brown, Commander of the U.S. Naval Force in the Pacific. Accepting the Admiral's hospitality, King Kalakaua sailed on November 25th, accompanied by his Chamberlain, Col. George W. Macfarlane, and his aide-de-camp, Major R. Hoapili Baker.

As the *Charleston* moved slowly out of Honolulu Harbour, a bad omen was seen by many Hawaiians; shoals of red *aweoweo* fish played around the water's edge. They were always harbingers of death for the *alii*.

Kalakaua's final *"Memorandum of Orders"* penned on the day prior to his departure for San Francisco, November 24th, 1890 read:

1. *See the Minister of Interior about Mausoleum.*
2. *Pay the school bills of Miss Leleo and Kehaulani.*
3. *See Kaanaana and Niaulani . . . Liloy now at Hilo.*
4. *Give the usual payments to Jos. Liliwai of fifty-three dollars per week.*
5. *Put a telephone in Aiea to connect with the city.*
6. *Make J. Bowler or his man to go down Aiea to plaster the bath place.*
7. *Furnish the boys at Aiea with one barrel poi weekly and salmon when required. They have already a barrel of beef.*

Kalakaua
Nov. 24/90.

Meanwhile, the inevitable rumours flew that the King was going to the mainland to arrange Annexation of Hawaii to the U.S. at this time.

The New York Tribune published a direct despatch from its San Francisco office supporting the Annexation story. Soon speculation joined in from as far afield as Canada where Col. V.V. Ashford was negotiating trade and predicting imminent Annexation, as well as from London, England. Back home in Honolulu *The Pacific Commercial-Advertiser* printed an editorial on December 31, 1890, denying the rumours: *"There is not the first word of truth in it regarding the King's mission. . ."*

Liliuokalani mentioned in her book, *Hawaii's Story by Hawaii's Queen* that when her brother, Kalakaua came to see her three days before his departure for the United States, she did all she could to dissuade him from going:

". . . But the principal motive of his journey was to have an interview with Mr. H.A.P. Carter, the Hawaiian Minister at Washington, in order to give him instructions in view of the McKinley Bill, which had just passed the American Congress, the influence of which was supposed to be dangerous to the interest of the foreign element at Honolulu, and destructive to the profits of the sugar planters. . ."

In a feature story published by *The San Francisco Chronicle* in December 1890 it was reported that King Kalakaua was *". . . working on a theological book that will startle the world. . . "*

King Kalakaua sailing for San Francisco on the *Charleston*, November 1890.

On December 4th, the *Charleston* arrived in San Francisco where a crowd of thousands cheered the King as he came ashore. At four o'clock that afternoon Kalakaua was officially escorted to the Palace Hotel.

In a letter dated January 1, 1891, Kalakaua wrote his impressions to James W. Robertson in Honolulu:

". . . A spontaneous ovation. I have never seen the like before. Not one moment's rest. Travelling day and night. Receptions, balls, dinners, dinners, Masonic initiations. . . Sunshine, rain, storm, etc. . . it's all the same. Wonder that I am not half dead yet. Anyhow everything has its effect. . . and I have learnt and have seen a great deal. Nice country. Good people and all that but awfully damn cold. Whio!"

On January 4, 1891, when the King's Party reached Santa Barbara returning from the Southern California tour, the first symptoms of the King's illness were noticed.

Admiral Brown observed during the day that:*". . . The King's mind was dull. . . and he was not in a normal condition. . ."*

Dr. G.N. Woods, Medical Inspector on the *Charleston* later wrote his report on the King's illness to Hon. John Cummins: "*. . . On the morning of Monday, the 5th inst., an excursion was made with the Mayor and others to Cooper's Ranch distant twelve miles from Santa Barbara. The same conditions being noticed by Admiral Brown as on the previous evening he requested Dr. McNulty, one of the entertaining party to ride in the carriage with His Majesty. During the trip, a constant disposition was manifested to fall asleep, and both on the way, and in viewing Mr. Cooper's beautiful estate, an entire in-difference to all that was shown him. At luncheons he indulged in no conver-sation, fell asleep repeatedly, but when aroused, was coherent, though sluggish in his speech. . .*"

By now it was decided that Kalakaua needed medical attention. His tra-velling party returned to the Palace Hotel in San Francisco where the King was put to bed and attended by Dr. McNulty.

On Wednesday the 14th of January, the King was in a lethargic condition, but nothing would deter him from attending a Masonic Order ceremonial that evening where he was to introduce *"The Mystic Shrine."* Kalakaua's serious condition was explained to him, but his only answer was: "*. . . I must go. . . and nothing shall prevent me from going.*"

During the day he slept constantly and indulged in no conversation. When roused, his only thought was of the evening ceremony, and he would murmur, "*I must go. . . I must go to the Shrine. . .*"

At 8:30 the Masonic Committee conducted Kalakaua to the Temple. The King was placed in the charge of his old friend General Dimond who promised that His Majesty should be submitted to no shock or fatiguing cere-monies and should be back at his apartments within an hour, which promise was faithfully kept.

Kalakaua's condition worsened.

The doctors gave their diagnosis: *"Interstitial nephritis with uraemia"* also the *"heart was largely hypertrophied and the liver contracted. . . a con-dition probably due to cirrhosis."*

By Monday, January 19, the King was almost completely in a coma. Communion services of the Protestant Episcopal Church were conducted in his suite by the Rev. F.H. Church.

By Tuesday morning, the King's strength was only maintained by brandy and glycerine trickled into his mouth from a drop tube.

Dr. Woods noted: *"There were present at this moment, at the bedside, on the right of His Majesty. . . Rev. Mr. Reed, Col. Macfarlane and Admiral Brown. . . on the left, Col. Baker, Kalua and Kahikina. . . and at the foot of the bed, Mrs. Swan, Consul McKinley and Medical Inspector Woods. Grouped around were Lieut. Dyer, Hon. C.R. Bishop, Mr. Godfrey Rhodes, Judge Hart, Sen. G.E. Whitney, Mrs. McKinley, Mrs. Price, Mrs. J. Sanders Reed and the Hon Claus Spreckels."*

Rev. J. Sanders Reed recited passages from the scriptures and the Rev. Mr. Church led the singing of hymns.

"At the last," wrote Dr. Woods, *"this service was changed to prayer, all kneeling, the words of devotion mingling with His Majesty's last breath. At 2:35 p.m. on Tuesday, January 20th, 1891, His Majesty Kalakaua I. of the Kingdom of Hawaii. . . ceased to exist. . ."*

The last photo of Kalakaua. . . taken by Thomas C. Marceau of San Francisco, in early January 1891.

Dr. Woods ended his report to John Cummins: *"Finally, I feel it my duty to express my earnest appreciation of the services. . . and the kind and loving attention bestowed by His Majesty's Hawaiian servants upon their sovereign. It was perfect in its character. . . such as no foreign servants could have given, rendering the presence of the trained nurse almost superfluous. . . and both soothing and comforting in the highest degree, their native words at last, being all His Majesty could comprehend. . ."*

Photo courtesy Sheraton Palace Hotel, San Francisco

The historic Garden Court of the Palace Hotel (now the Sheraton Palace) is shown in this early picture as it appeared before the earthquake and fire of 1906. It was then a palatial carriage courtyard entrance. When the hotel was rebuilt, the courtyard was covered and today the Garden Court of the Sheraton Palace is a fashionable meeting place for breakfast, lunch and buffet dinner. Many have called it *"the most beautiful dining room in the world."*

The fascinating prospect that the voice of King David Kalakaua, last of the Hawaiian Kings, may be heard again, has long been discussed since there exists a recording the King made during his last days.

In August 1936 *The Honolulu Advertiser* printed the following account by George Macfarlane, first published in *Paradise of the Pacific*, February, 1891:

". . . While he lies abed too weak to even raise his great frame, two solicitous attendants hover about the suite. They are his aide-de-camps; blonde Chamberlain, George Macfarlane and swarthy Major Robert Hoapili Baker.

By the King's bedside, a queer contrivance stands. A few days before, a man had come and presented it to Chamberlain Macfarlane. The man was Louis Glass, he said, and represented the Edison Phonograph Co. and he explained the contrivance as a recording machine. He wanted. . . if it would please His Majesty. . . to have the King's voice recorded. The phonograph was something new. . . invented just a few years before by one Thomas Edison and the recording of the King's voice might aid in publicizing the instrument. Would the King from Hawaii perhaps aid? Macfarlane had told him he would try, but that at present the King was a very ill man. So for several days the queer instrument. . . a mouthpiece contrivance with wax cylinder and sensitive metal arm pointed with steel needle. . . stood by Kalakaua's bed. Macfarlane had explained to the King what it was and why it was there.

On this day, January 16, Kalakaua decides that it might be a good idea to try it out. It would be nice to say a few words, and if it really did work like Glass had explained, have these words reproduced in Hawaii for his people. So they move the instrument closer to the bed. Glass has been called to operate the device. Gently, they raise the wasted King in his bed. He adjusts the ear receivers and speaks into the instrument. He speaks slowly, pausing long for breath. He speaks in Hawaiian: 'Aloha kaua,' he says with great effort. Then, 'Aloha kaua,' again. 'Ke hoi nei no paha makou ma keia hope aku i Hawaii i Honolulu. A ilaila oe e hai aku ai oe i ka lehulehu i kau mea e lohe ai ianei.'

'Greetings to you. Greetings to you. We will very likely hereafter go to Hawaii, to Honolulu. There you will tell my people what you have heard me say here. . .'

He has spoken directly to the machine as if reproduction were some power within the apparatus itself; as if there were some rationality there. Then he sinks back exhausted.

The machine is left in the suite, for it is hoped that the King later will say some more. But Kalakaua never spoke into the machine again. . ."

The Advertiser reported on February 20th, 1891, that one W.H. Aldrich had arrived on the steamer *Zealandia*, bearing the King's record for Chamberlain Macfarlane. It was to be entrusted to the Queen Dowager Kapiolani, and to be played only with her consent.

Col. Macfarlane gave the cylinder to one J.W. Pratt sometime in 1891, because Pratt observed, he (Pratt) *". . . happened to have the only phonograph machine in the Hawaiian Kingdom."* He said that the recording was very faint and quite squeaky. He continued to remark that Liliuokalani had heard the record reproduced, but that Queen Kapiolani refused to hear it played.

As of this writing the badly damaged wax cylinder is still undergoing restoration work in a laboratory in the Eastern U.S.

In a letter written to the late newspaperman Clark Lee, Columnist Ashton Stevens recalled a party he attended as a young man in Kalakaua's suite at the Palace Hotel:

"Kalakaua was the only King I ever met. I met him through Will Unger. . . Captain of the King's Guard when Hawaii was a high rolling Monarchy. Kalakaua had come to San Francisco for medical advice. Champagne as a steady irrigator had wrecked his kidneys. It was still wrecking them the night Will Unger inducted me and my banjo into King Kalakaua's spacious suite in S.F.'s Palace Hotel.

The proceedings were rather formal at first, doubtless in deference to the presence of our navy's high brass. The King, a bronze personality whose dignity was overmatched only by his magnetic amiability, sat in a high backed chair atop a small carpeted platform. His glass was lifted often and filled often. . . as were our own.

It was not until the Navy had made its midnight departure that the night became truly Hawaiian. Then the King's Aide, Baker magically produced the King's favourite dancing girl, and with her gravely executed what was described to us as the Royal Hula-hula. It was a chaste and comely measure softly accompanied by native ukulele, taropatch and the Spanish guitar.

Kalakaua's retainers: Kalua at lower left, Ahi Niu, Kapihekawelo, Victoria Akuua.

Bishop Museum

Another glass of Monopole and I was commanded to sit in a small chair beside the King and sound my utensil. I think His Majesty allowed me an encore following another bumper of Champagne. His manner now suggested free speech. . . and my innocency emboldened, I asked him how it felt to be a King. He graciously answered that it didn't feel so good to be a King, as it used to before the Missionaries got to plaguing him with embarrassing reforms for his people. No more Sunday picnics, no more all-night hulas, no more gin. The Missionaries, he said, had taken almost all the fun out of being a King. 'I'd like to sing. . . if you gentlemen will sing with me. . .' he presently announced. . . and we joined him in barbershopping the one that starts: 'I cannot bear to leave thee!'

He led us in a good clear tenor that slowed up sentimentally when the harmony found a true tonsorial.

Kalakaua liked to sing. . . and we liked his singing. . . and the singing lasted till dawn. My last groggy memory is of kneeling while he bent down and decorated me by pinning a Monopole cork to the shirt bosom he had autographed. . . and bade me arise: 'Sir Knight of the Twinking Banjo.'

That was Kalakaua's last great feast. He died shortly after it. There was a solemn procession down Market St. to the waterfront as his body was borne to the U.S. Man-of-war chosen to carry it home to its Island tomb.

Fifty feet behind the slow, plumed hearse, veiled from crown to sole in black crepe, marched the dead monarch's dancing girl. . . alone.''

The following is an eye-witness account by Mr. T. Hayden Treadway of the return of the *Charleston* on January 29th, 1891, bearing the King's body home to the Islands:

". . . Honolulu rejoiced and wore gala dress. The Charleston *was due. The King was to return. Flags and pennants fluttered in the soft trade-winds; banners bore messages of aloha; arches of welcome had been erected over the route His Majesty would take on his way from the wharf to the Palace. No radio, wireless nor cable then gave us communication with the outside world. Yet we knew that news of the* Charleston's *return would be spread in ample time for expectant crowds to gather along the waterfront to welcome the monarch home.*

Well, we knew that thanks to our reliable "Diamond Head Charlie," the first glimpe of the distant cruiser would be reported to town by telephone. . . and the news would spread like wildfire. . . as news does in small communities.

Everyone who has seen pictures of Honolulu is familiar with Diamond Head, the grand old volcanic sentinel that stands guard over the entrance to our port. The keeper of the lighthouse there was a trusted and beloved old man (old to us youngsters at least) Charles Peterson. Few, I think, knew that his name was Peterson. He was Diamond Head Charlie. . . and nary a vessel came within the scope of his vision without being immediately reported. . . Never had Charlie watched for a vessel with greater expectancy than on this day. He knew that a word from him would be the signal for fresh flowers and ferns and palm leaves to be added to the welcoming decorations that had begun two weeks before. . .

And there at last was the Charleston, *slowly coming into view! He levelled his strong telescope upon the ship. . . and was aghast! It couldn't be true. Flags were at half-mast. There could be but one explanation. The King was dead.*

Gloom spread where all had been so gay. Colourful decorations were hastily removed, giving place to sombre black. Stores were ransacked for their stock of black crepe. Many a sleeve was to wear a band of this material for some time to come. . .

I shall never forget the scene at the wharf; the quiet throng; soldiers drawn up, ready to escort the King's remains. The steamers of that day were coal burners, and great hills of black, black coal stood near the place where they docked.

Now the barge from the Charleston *neared the landing. From the crowd emerged a white-haired Hawaiian woman. She was thin and bent and barefoot. She wore a neat black* holoku *(mother hubbard) and an old fashioned hat of Hawaiian* lauhala *braid. Unassisted, she climbed to*

The landing of King Kalakaua's body from the U.S.S. *Charleston*.

the top of the largest pile of coal. There she stood, a slender, dark silhouette against the clear sunny sky. Now the coffin was lifted from the barge. With a queenly, graceful motion, she raised her right arm high above her head. Then in the rich resonant voice of the Polynesian, she began to wail. Her chanting was a wail. . . and her wailing was a chant. No one who has ever heard Hawaiian wailing for the dead can, I think, fail to experience a half-shuddering thrill at the memory of it. Syllables gushed over syllables in the soft Hawaiian language, as she eulogized Kalakaua and recounted the deeds of his ancestors, with poetic reference, now and then to the grandeur and beauty of Nature. Then the wailing would come to a great crescendo, gradually growing softer until the notes wavered and died away, sometimes broken by a sob. . .

The coffin was reverently placed upon a horse drawn truck that had been suitably draped. With its escort the vehicle started for the Palace. Army, Navy and official personnel were followed by civilians. . . heading towards Ewa (roughly speaking, West). That is not a direction from which we ever expect showers, and the sky was clear and bright, with no sign of mist; but noting the murmur around me and following the glance of others I looked up and saw that we were walking directly towards the arch of the grandest, brightest rainbow that I had ever seen. It seemed like a gateway opening to us. . .

The procession took a right turn. . . up Fort Street. . . a course at right angles to our first. . . yet there directly in front of us, calling to us . . . was the rainbow. It remained undimmed. . . until we reached the corner of King Street. There must be another radical turn. . . but the splendid arch still faced us as we turned our way towards Kaimuki. . . exactly opposite from the position where it had first appeared. At no time did we see two rainbows. . . and at no time did we see one move. It was just there. . . bidding us come to its splendid arch. . . leading us at each turn. . .

Kalakaua's casket on the U.S.S. *Charleston*.

The great Palace gates were open to receive what had been earthly of the monarch who had so often driven between their pillars with the prancing horses and the liveried attendants, that bespoke his position. We turned again and entered the Royal gates. Now, as on our way up Fort Street, we were facing the beautiful range of mountains that was the background of Honolulu. And arched magnificently above them was our rainbow!

On the balcony that overlooked the front steps, our bereaved Queen, the beloved Kapiolani, had taken her place with the ladies of her court to look down upon a scene far different from the joyous home-coming she had anticipated. . .

It was about five o'clock when the procession entered the gates. The beautiful rainbow maintained its watch until dusk.

'Auwe!' cried the people. ' He alii oia i'o no ka o Kalakaua!' 'Kala-kaua is indeed an alii!'"

The next day, January 30, 1891, the Princess Regent Liliuokalani was summoned to Iolani Palace. In the Blue Room members of the Cabinet, the Privy Council and the Supreme Court solemnly awaited her.

Chief Justice Judd said they had come to administer the oath of office. Later Liliuokalani wrote in her book: *"I asked why the proceedings could not be deferred until after my brother's funeral, but ere I realized what was involved, I was compelled to take the oath to the Constitution ... the institution of which had brought about the death of my brother. . ."*

An *"acknowledgment"* from Queen Kapiolani to U.S.S. *Charleston.*

"The nation feels her sorrow is deeper than mere words," wrote *The Bulletin "He was a true and loyal King. He died as he had lived, with an eye single to national advancement."*

Queen Kapiolani kneeling at Kalakaua's casket. . . Throne Room, Iolani Palace.

On February 15th funeral services were conducted by Rt. Rev. Alfred Willis, Episcopal Bishop of Honolulu. . . in the Throne Room of Iolani Palace.

The golden feather cloak of Kamehameha lay over Kalakaua's casket while *kahilis* stood majestically on all sides. At the head of the casket Queen Kapiolani sat quietly with her head bowed.

As the funeral procession moved out of the Palace grounds, torch bearers followed the King's black horse (with saddle reversed) up the valley to the Royal Mausoleum at Nuuanu. One hundred and fifty Native Sons of Hawaii drew the catafalque, all stevedores, for this was their privilege. Long supported by the King, tearful members of the Hawaiian Societies came to bid farewell to their Monarch. Ho'oulu Lahui and Ka Lei Mamo were there. High Priest Auld of Ka Hale Naua carried the sacred calabash, a feather helmet and a tabu stick.

After the services Auld placed the calabash on Kalakaua's casket, then moved quickly away, weeping.

Four large kahilis were stuck into the ground before the tomb where they remained until the last feather was carried away on the wind.

Dan Logan, editor of the *Bulletin* wrote: *"The torch that burns at midday has been quenched. . ."*

Kalakaua's funeral procession. Two hundred native sons of Hawaii drawing the cataflaque.

Bishop Museum

Royal standard behind photo of King.

Liliuokalani expressed her deep feelings for her brother: *". . . So the King went cheerfully and patiently to work for the cause of those who had been and were his enemies. . . . He sacrificed himself in the interests of the very people who had done him so much wrong, and given him such constant suffering.*

"With an ever-forgiving heart he forgot his own sorrows, set aside all feelings of animosity, and to the last breath of his life he did all that lay in his power for those who had abused and injured him. . .

"If ever there was a man who was pure in spirit, if ever there was a mortal who had perfect charity, he was that man. In spite of all the revilings uttered against him, he never once opened his lips to speak against another, whomsoever it might be. And so my poor brother said goodbye to us all. . . and bade farewell to his beautiful Islands, which he was never to look on again. . ."

King Kalakaua's will named his sister Liliuokalani as heir to the Throne. She ruled until the Monarchy's overthrow in 1893 by the very people whose unbridled ambitions Kalakaua had struggled to control during his entire reign.

Kalakaua's niece Princess Kaiulani was next in line of succession and: *". . . the heirs of her body. In succession it being our wish and desire that the sovereignship of the Kingdom of Hawaii be perpetuated in the family of which we are the head. . ."*

The fourth article of the King's will stated that if the throne should descend to Princess Kaiulani before *"she attained the age of majority"* the Queen Consort Kapiolani would rule.

In the sixth article the King continued:

"It is our wish that when the last one of our immediate family shall come to the throne, there being no issue of his or her body to succeed in order, and Her Majesty the Queen Kapiolani not being alive when such event shall occur, the throne of Hawaii shall descend to our beloved sister Her Royal Highness Princess Poomaikelani and after her, failing heirs of her body, the throne of Hawaii shall descend in order to the sons of our cousin as follows, first, to His Royal Highness Prince David Kawananakoa and to the heirs of his body; and failing heirs then to His Royal Highness Prince Cupid Kalanianaole and the heirs of his body; each to assume the name and title of Kalakaua, and to be numbered in order from us as the first of this name in case no male heir to the throne shall have assumed this name, and in that case to assume the number that shall next follow in numerical order. . . ."

FINIS

The Hawaiian Historical Society

Queen Kapiolani (right) beside Kalakaua's casket. Throne room, Iolani Palace.

Bishop Museum

Kalakaua's funeral at Royal Mausoleum.

Photo of King taken just before his death in San Francisco.

Throne Room, Iolani Palace. Included in photo are: Mr. Widemann, Mrs. Sam Parker, Col. Curtis Iaukea, Hon. John Dominis, Mrs. Haalelea, Charles Clark.

Reconstruction of Iolani Palace dining room, in Kalakaua's time.

Reconstruction of table setting. Kalakaua's dining room, Iolani Palace.

Breakfast at Iolani Palace

IN HONOR OF

Mr and Mrs E. E. Thorne

MAY 21, 1883.

Menu.

Fruit.

Fried Mullet.   Boiled Kumu.

Beef Steak,   Mutton Chops,

Pork Chops,   Poached Eggs,

Broiled Chicken,   Pigeon on Toast,

Kidney, with Tomato Sauce,   Chicken Curry,

Omlette.

Tea,   Coffee.

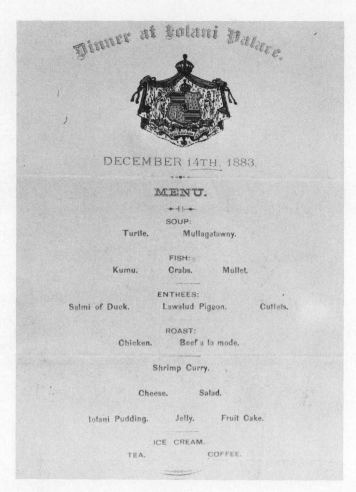

Dinner at Iolani Palace.

DECEMBER 14TH, 1883.

MENU.

SOUP:

Turtle.   Mullagatawny.

FISH:

Kumu.   Crabs.   Mullet.

ENTREES:

Salmi of Duck.   Lawalud Pigeon.   Cutlets.

ROAST:

Chicken.   Beef a la mode.

Shrimp Curry.

Cheese.   Salad.

Iolani Pudding.   Jelly.   Fruit Cake.

ICE CREAM.

TEA.   COFFEE.

Samples of Palace menus.

There were many formal dinners held at Iolani Palace such as the one in 1889 given by the King for the Commander and Officers of the *USS Nipsic*. It was held in the State Dining Room, while the Royal Hawaiian Military Band, as it was sometimes called, stationed outside on the verandah, played waltzes, polkas and gavottes during the evening for guests elegantly attired in full evening dress and decorations.

A simple menu consisted of mock turtle soup and soup a la reine, boiled *kumu* and fried mullet, oyster pates, salmi of duck and pigeon on toast for entrees, a pause for Roman Punch, then turkey, fillet of beef and ham, shrimp and chicken curry, salad and cheese, mashed potatoes, green peas and saratoga potatoes, asparagus and mushrooms and finally pudding, ice cream, fruit, coffee, "*segars*" and liqueurs. . . .

Silver pieces - Dining Room, Iolani Palace - Kalakaua's reign.

The Throne Room - Iolani Palace - 1880's.

Stairway inside Iolani Palace.

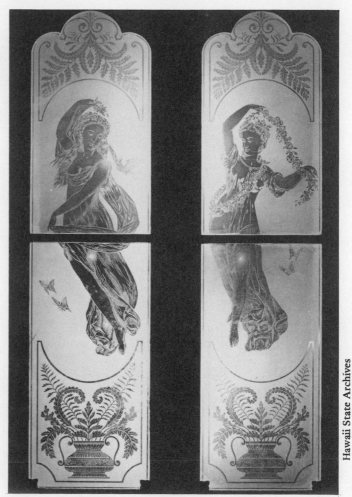

Glass door panels inside Iolani Palace.

King Kalakaua also enjoyed entertaining at breakfast, served at eleven o'clock in the morning. The breakfast menus were much the same as for the dinners with only *"segars"* and liqueurs omitted.

Not only was the food bountiful at Iolani Palace, the decorations were equally lavish. At another dinner in honour of the Commander-In-Chief of the U.S. Pacific Fleet, Rear-Admiral George Brown, forty-two gentlemen sat down to the table. The centerpiece was an anchor of roses three feet in length, shaded from deep red to white, placed on a crimson silk plush ground. Two large silver candelabra, each with twenty five candles, lighted the table, supplemented by *"pretty fairy lamps."* This particular dinner was held on a hot August evening, and the guests wore heavy, full dress dinner clothes.

The King's bed - Iolani Palace.

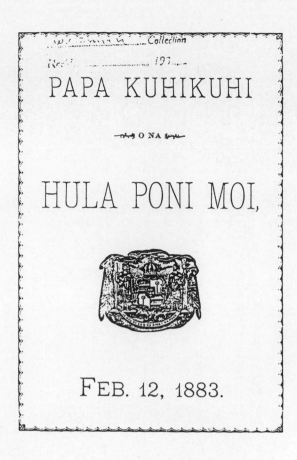

IOANE.

KOIHONUA—KAI WAWAE MAMUA.

1. Ike ia Haehae..........................Hula Ku'i
2. Ike ia Kaukini........................   "   "
3. I aloha i ka lau Oliva................   "   "
4. Hookahi pua e kau nei..............Hula Ukeke
5. Malama i ka Haku a he pua...........   "   "
6. Auhea wale oe e ke Kona............   "   "
7. Nani wale no Maemae...............   "   "
8. Ia oe e ka La e alohi nei..............Hula Ulili
9. Anoai i ke Aloha......................   "   "
10. Kuupau lia mai.......................   "   "
11. Ee aku o Kalani......................   "   "
12. A Kona Hema o Kalani...............   "   "
13. Aole i piliwi ia.......................Hula Paipu
14. Auhea wale ana oe...................   "   "

Excerpts from the King's *"Offensive" Hula Programme* performed on Coronation Day, February 12, 1883.

KAONOWAI.

Li mai Kalani Li Kalapana . . . . Mele Oli

Kaulilua i ke anu Waialeale . . . .   "   Ku'i

Anoai ke Aloha na Lai a Ehu . . . .   "   "

Loe Kuaiwa o Laa ke Alii . . . .   "   Oli

Ua poniia o Davida i ka la umi-kumalua . . . . .   "   Ku'i

Ua poniia o Davida imua o ke Akua Mana Loa   "   "

Ke ai la Kalani i ka paka . . . . Kielei

Hanalei aiua kukele i ka ua . . . .   "

O Mana aina kumuwai i Kalani . . . .   "

Poniu Kona i ka la . . . . Aihaa

A la, wela Kona . . . .   "

Kupilikii Hanalei he ua la . . . .   "

Holo ana Kalakaua imi i ka Pono o na Moku . . . .   "

Aloha mai ka hoa mai pelekane . . . .   "

Na Kane i hee ka nalu o Oahu . . . .   "

Kaulilua i ke anu Waialeale . . . .   "

Ulili walaau ka manu i ka wai . . . . Mele Oli

Ua poni ia o Davida i ka la umi kumalua . . . . Ulili

Ua poni ia o Davida imua o ke Akua Mana Loa . . .   "

O ka wana halula . . . . Mele Oli

Ua poni ia o Davida i ka la umi kumalua . . Paiumauma

Ua poni ia o Davida imua o ke Akua Mana Loa   "

S. Ua.

Oi oe o ka mole uaua o ke'lii................Mele Oli
A luna wau o Kaimuki...................Hula Paipu
Ia oe e ka La e alohi nei................ "   "
E ala e Hawaii o Keawe.....................Aihaa

O aua ia e Kama ko na moku...............Mele Oli
Ka nalu nui e ku, ka nalu mai Kona.......Hula Paipu
Noho aku o Kalani i ka olu............... "   "
Aole i manao ia, kahi wai o Alekoki............Aihaa

Ka nalu nui e ku, ka nalu mai Kona.........Mele Oli
Hulihia Kilauea po i ka uahi............Hula Paipu
Ke amo la ke koi, ke kua la iuka......Aihaa (2 pauku)

Kaulilua i ke anu Waialeale.................Mele Oli
A ke poo o Puna i Puna ka makani........Hula Paipu
He lua i Kahiki ua aina e Pele........Aihaa (6 pauku)
Ko mai kiliopu, ke papani aku la..........Hula Paipu

A Koholalele pau ka ino a ka makani.........Mele Oli
Aia i Haili ko lei nani.........{ Hula Paipu (7 pauku)
                                { (Elua Aihaa)

Kiekie Kau hanohano i ka makani...........Mele Oli
Aia i ka hikina ko kapa..........Hula Paipu (2 pauku)
Aia i ka hoku ko kapa......................Aihaa

O Ulihiwa i ka lani na Uli...................Mele Oli
Ke hele mai nei ke Kuini................Hula Paipu
Auhea wale oe e ka ua.......................Aihaa

Nani wale ka liko o ia pua...............Hula Paipu
Kaulana ke anu i kanahele.....................Aihaa
Kahiko ka nani i Iolani..................Hula Paipu
Kahiko ka nani i Lauhulu.....................Aihaa

Hoouna ka Elele, kii e ka La................Mele Oli
O Kalauohua ka manu alii...............Hula Paipu
Hookumu ka Lani, kumu ka Honua.............Aihaa

He Inoa nou e Kapiii............................
Pualei a Makue.......................Hula Paipu
Pali mai Waipio i ka noe.....................Aihaa

"On the twenty-fourth day of September, 1886, by request from the king, a charter was granted by the privy council to the Hale Naua, or Temple of Science. Probably some of its forms had been taken by my brother from the Masonic ritual, and others may have been taken from the old and harmless ceremonies of the ancient people of the Hawaiian Islands, which were then only known to the priests of the highest orders. Under the work of this organization was embraced matters of science known to historians, and recognized by the priests of our ancient times. The society further held some correspondence with similar scientific associations in foreign lands, to whom it communicated its proceedings. The result was some correspondence with those bodies, who officially accepted the theories propounded by the Hale Naua; and in recognition of this acceptance medals were sent from abroad to the members highest in rank in the Hawaiian society. Unworthy and unkind reflections have been made on the purposes of this society by those who knew nothing of it. Persons with mean and little minds can readily assign false motives to actions intended for good, and attribute to lofty ideas a base purpose or unholy intention. That some good has been done by this organization the members themselves could readily certify. It had been the custom before the days of His Majesty Kalakaua (it is the usage even to the present day) for the chiefs to support the destitute and to bury the dead. This society opened to them an organized method of doing this; it cared for the sick, and it provided for the funerals of the dead. Had the king lived, more good would have been done, and the society would have been in a more flourishing condition; yet the money contributed for its purposes while he lived was invested in stocks, and many persons have drawn benefits from the dividends. Although it was small, it was a beginning."

From "Hawaii's Story by Hawaii's Queen, Liliuokalani."

EXCERPTS FROM THE HALE NAUA

deferred to some other nights, which nights are those of Hua, Akua, Hoku, Mahealani and Lono. All special sessions of the Sanctuary will sit on the following nights: Hilo (new moon), Hoaka (second night), the four *Ku* nights, the nights of Huna, Mohalu, the three nights of Laau and three nights of Kaloa.

ARTICLE IX . . . .

Each officer is selected annually. The announcement of the election is made by the presentation of the black pebble for the negative and the white for the affirmative. If both stones are exhibited, the sign is doubtful. The member doubting can cast his or her vote to whatever side he or she chooses to vote. A majority of black or white stones exhibited will decide the member or officer elected for the next ensuing year. The votes are first brought to the knowledge of the Iku Hai or presiding officer who will pronounce the same to the members in a loud and audible voice.

ARTICLE X . . . .

Each member should be posted with the ritual and to understand the moral lessons and the principles it inculcates, after commitment to memory to burn its contents; all oaths are kept and not desecrated until the oracle is closed.

ARTICLE XI . . . .

The Seal of the Order or Society shall be same in every respect with that of the Banner. Having the figure of the sun, the cross, the motto and the additional words of Hawaii, date, month and year of its establishment in the ancient idiom of the Order. The seal is represented as follows, viz:

ARTICLE XII . . . .

No member is eligible to hold a diploma unless he or she has passed the Fifth Degree of the Order.

ARTICLE XIII . . . .

All important cases of irregularities are fairly tried and heard before the Iku Hai or Presiding Officer, who will preside as Chief Arbitrator in the cases of disagreement among its members, or trial for all offenses and misdemeanor.

ARTICLE XIV . . . .

No member is allowed to attend the meeting if he or she is in any way indisposed. Such as are indisposed

and unable to attend for the payment of his or her dues, fines or penalties, shall have the privilege of being represented by proxy, who will state the cause and reason for the absence or ailments of the member absent.

ARTICLE XV

The diploma shall certify his or her membership, age and character, signed by the Iku Hai or Presiding Officer, and countersigned by the Secretary. The charges on diplomas shall be two dollars ($2.00), made upon parchment, and delivered on his or her taking the degree of membership.

ARTICLE XVI

This Constitution is amendable to change at the regular session or meeting of the Society mentioned in Article VIII.

BY-LAWS
... OF THE ... ...

Hale Naua or ....
Temple of Science

✚

SECTION I.

There are nine degrees of the Order and are marked in the following order.

- 1st. Preliminary.
- 2d. Instructive.
- 3d. Preparatory.
- 4th. Operative.
- 5th. Pass to membership and eligible to receive diplomas.
- 6th. The signs of the Aliis or chiefs.
- 7th. The close or conclusion of the Ancient degree.
- 8th. Christian Degree.
- 9th. Order of the Golden Ribbon or Temperance degree.

SECTION II.

No person can become a member if he or she is over 65 years of age, and not in vigorous health. Children under 10 years of age are admitted in the Preliminary degree; but the parents shall hold themselves responsible for their good conduct, behavior and standing.

Section III

At regular and special sessions only those of lawful age and who have attained their degree of membership are allowed to attend.

Section IV

At all public ceremonials of the order, the Grand Honors are only given to the Iku Hai or Presiding officer, and those who have passed the Presidential Chair.

Section V

The Banner of the Society with those of the members, the field is Yellow, edged with Red; and the figure of the Sun mounted upon a Cross, with the name of the society, "Hale Naua," affixed thereto. The Banner of the Society and those of the members is represented as follows, viz.:

Section VI

The Flag of the Order shall be White, Red and Yellow Colors, alternately of equal stripes; the device of the Banner with the motto being placed in the center as is placed in the Banner of the Order. The Pennant is of a similar pattern with colors on the head of the pennant, and each member is entitled to a Banner of ancient devices and placed at the back of his or her seat. On the back of his or her seat his or her feather cape is placed; the apron or malo and other paraphernalia in which he or she is to clothe before they take their seats are in the room of the Sanctuary.

Section VII

At the second entrance of the room are two Puloulou which are named Kialoa and Kiaakapoko, signifying wisdom and strength. Two Kahilis on each side of the throne are emblematic of fire and water, the two greatest emblems of purification.

Section VIII

On the northern corner which is designated the House of Papa, are placed three Drums, their names are Kamau, Lono, and Niuaola. The session of the Sanctuary is represented as follows, viz.:

Section IX

All Honors of Dignity and Orders are invested, bestowed and conferred by a special dispensation granted by the Iku Hai or Sovereign of the Sanctuary, called for that specific purpose.

Section X

All persons contributing $50.00 are entitled to Honorary life membership, and rank in the Fifth Class of honors, and are entitled to Decoration of that class. At $100 they are entitled to the same privilege and receive decorations of the Fourth order, and so forth up to the higher degrees of rank. The Kahilis and Puloulou and the Malo or cordon are only granted under dispensation by the Iku Hai. All honorary members are expected to send contributions upon any subject of Scientific interest, Art and Literature. There shall be two standing committees: One on the Investigation of the character of the applicant and the other for the approval of admittance after the Investigation Committee had reported.

Section XI

The Heralds shall lead the procession unless otherwise ordered to the center or rear. The band or drums and trumpets (coock shells) following their movements unless otherwise ordered.

Section XII

The Master of the Ceremonies shall marshall and direct all ceremonials and shall assign duties to those who have obtained their membership to his assistance.

SECTION XX . . .

ORDER AND PROCEEDINGS
OF BUSINESS

1. Reading of the Minutes.
2. Reports of Committees.
3. Unfinished Business.
4. New Business.
5. Election of Members.
6. Collections of Fees, Dues, Fines and Penalties.
7. Initiation or Degrees.

SECTION XXI . . . . .

The members shall have in memory the ancient designation of the nights of the different phases of the moon of each month, which are as follows, viz :

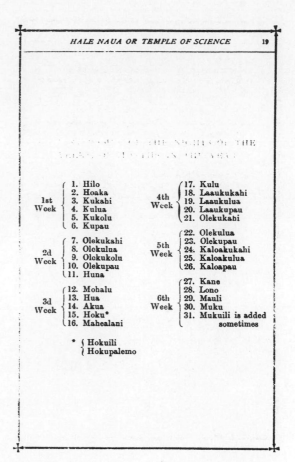

	1. Hilo		17. Kulu
1st Week	2. Hoaka	4th Week	18. Laaukukahi
	3. Kukahi		19. Laaukulua
	4. Kulua		20. Laaukupau
	5. Kukolu		21. Olekukahi
	6. Kupau		
	7. Olekukahi		22. Olekulua
2d Week	8. Olekulua	5th Week	23. Olekupau
	9. Olokukolu		24. Kaloakukahi
	10. Olekupau		25. Kaloakulua
	11. Huna		26. Kaloapau
	12. Mohalu		27. Kane
3d Week	13. Hua	6th Week	28. Lono
	14. Akua		29. Mauli
	15. Hoku*		30. Muku
	16. Mahealani		31. Mukuili is added sometimes

* { Hokuili
   { Hokupalemo

---

burning by fire or, third, malicious intent and desecration without cause; fourth, or oath or by the advice or instigation of another or others. Their oracles or any of the paraphernalia belong thereto, they will be fined by the rules of the Hale Lau and Imu Loa, as follows, viz :

A. 1st Degree equivalent to Twenty Dollars fine....$20 00
B. 2d   "   "   " Thirty   "   " 30 00
C. 3d   "   "   " Fifty   "   " 50 00
D. 4th   "   "   " Sixty   "   " 60 00

The degrees of punishment in accordance to the nature of the offense committed, under the ancient manner and style are as follows :

Ancient Penalties

A. 1st degree, two hogs. The male at a yard length and the female sow and one bundle of awa and a Kumu.

E. 2d degree, two hogs. The male and female each a yard's length and one bundle of awa and a Kumu.

I. 3d degree, two hogs. The male at four feet length; a female sow, one dog and two bundles of awa and two Kumu.

O. 4th degree, to impose upon the aliis or chiefs of the Sanctuary, three hogs, length at four feet and two sows of same length, three bundles of awa and three Kumu.

The offenses thus enumerated are as follows, viz :

    1st degree.   For destruction.
    2d degree.   Burning by fire.
    3d degree.   Malicious intent, etc.
    4th degree.   Oath, etc., etc.

FORM OF
Application for Admission

Honolulu, ... *18*

To the IKU HAI,

    Aliis of the Sanctuary and
    Mamos of the Temple of Science.

Salutation :

    The undersigned respectfully apply for admission to your Honorable Order, and represents Him-Herself as being of lawful age, of humble disposition and a law-abiding subject, and is desirous of entering thereof, and to abide by the Rules and Regulations of your Order. I am,

    Yours very respectfully,

        _____
                 (Signature)

COMMITTEE OF
APPROVAL   { _____

COMMITTEE OF INVESTIGATION
AS TO THE CHARACTER OF   { _____
THE APPLICANT

FORM OF NOTICES

TO THE

+

Honolulu,   *18*

Salutation :

You are hereby notified that..........................
*meeting of the Mamos of the Temple of Science will
be held at their Sanctuary on the night of*
....*corresponding to the*.................
day of.......................*in the month of*......................
at................*P. M.*
     Respectfully yours,

*You are hereby notified that your Beneficiary
Dues to date amount to*.............*dollars.*

FORM OF

Application for Acceptance

"Temple of Science"

Honolulu,.............. *18*

....
(Sir or Madam)

On the night of.......................*of the month of*
............................*your application to become a member
of this Order was received, and upon recommenda-
tion of Investigable Committee, and due deliberation
taken by them, have been accepted. You are advised
to pay to the Secretary in advance Two Dollars,
($2.00) with the assurance that you are provided
with the following articles :*

1. *An Oracle*
2. *A Kauwila Wand*
3. *A Ball of Olona Cordage*
4. *A Fish (Maka-a)*
5. *A single Root of the "Lauloa" taro*
6. *Uniform. (White Suit or Dress)*

*When prepared with these materials, the Order
will then initiate you in the Two preliminary
degrees.*

     Signed.................................
                               SECRETARY

THE TWELVE ANCIENT HAWAIIAN SIGNS OF ZODIAC

EXPLANATION OF THE ANCIENT TWELVE SIGNS OF ZODIAC

No.	MONTHS.	PROVERBS CONNECTED WITH EACH MONTH	SIGNS	MEANING OF SIGNS	APPLICATION TO THE HUMAN SYSTEM	Common Months	
1	Nana...............	Fisherman's lines and tackles are constantly wet from frequent use and fishing.		A ball of fish-line signification of Patience.	Heart and Intrail	Aug.	Virgo
2	Welo.............	The tides and currents are turning. (Autumnal Equinox.)		Endurance and Perseverance—A Virgin	The Abdomen	Sept.	Libra
3	Ikiki..............	The heavens are impatient.		Scales.	Kidneys and Waist	Oct.	Scorpio
4	Kaaona.	The sugar-cane tops are stained by smoke.		The Apron or Malo of the deity Kane.	Private Parts	Nov.	Sagitarius
5	Kaulua..........	Pause the sun and pause the rain. (Winter solstice.)		Thrusting and guarding Spear.	The Thighs	Dec.	Capricornus
6	Ikuwa....	The heavy and constant peal of thunder.		Knees of the deity named the Four-eyed electricity of Heaven.	The Knees	Jan.	quarius
7	Hilina.............	The winds are variable.		Long necked gourd calabash of water.	The Knee Joint and Legs	Feb.	Piscis
8	Hilinehu.......	The season of white bait or similar species.		The white bait.	The Foot and Toes	Mar.	Aries
9	Hinaiaeleele	The gigantic Platypus.		Platypus.	Face and Head	Apr.	Taurius
0	Kaelo	Month or season of ensaring plover.		The Plover ensnaring net.	The Neck	May	Gemini
1	Welehu	The month that buried and preserved food is due. (Summer solstice.)		The twin deities Ku and Kane.	The Hands	June	Cancer
2	Makalii	The hot and warm days of Makalii.		The wandering of Ocean crabs "Kukuau" on shore or land.	The Breast	July	Leo

ANCIENT HAWAIIAN NAMES OF THE MONTHS
OF THE YEAR AND NUMBER OF DAYS
AND THE EQUIVALENT

1.	Nana	-	31 nights or po.	1.	August	31 days
2.	Welo	- -	30 " "	2.	September	30 "
3.	Ikiki	-	31 " "	3.	October	31 "
4.	Kaaona	-	30 " "	4.	November	30 "
5.	Kaulua	-	30 " "	5.	December	31 "
6.	Ikuwa	- -	32 " "	6.	January	31 "
7.	Hilina	-	30 " "	7.	February	28† "
8.	Hilinehu	-	30 " "	8.	March	31 "
9.	Hinaiaeleele		30 " "	9.	April	30 "
10.	Kaelo	- -	30 " "	10.	May	31 "
11.	Welehu	-	30 " "	11.	June	30 "
12.	Makalii	-	31 " "	12.	July	31 "

Equivalent to 365 nights or days in the year.

†29 days, Leap Year.

King Kalakaua and Queen Kapiolani
on postage stamps issued in 1882.

Coronation: From illustrated London Daily News, 1883.

Coins issued in
King Kalakaua's time.

Hawaiians were understandably upset
at the appearance of these five cent coins
in 1881. The motto was misspelled and Hawaii
was called *"The Sandwich Islands."*

Kalakaua's eyeglasses

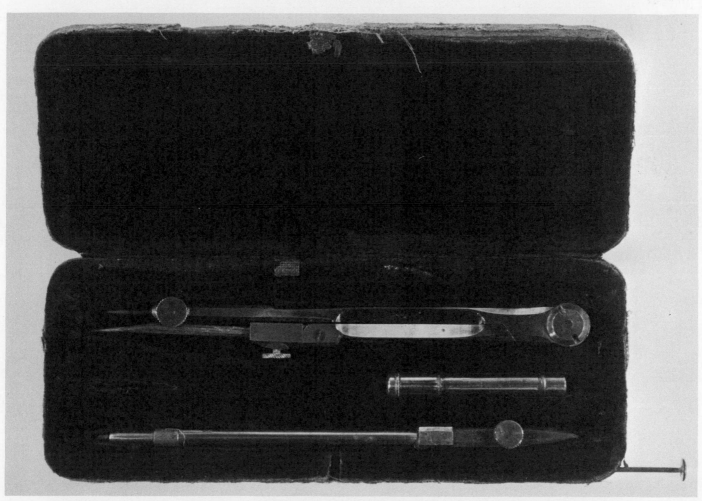

The King's drawing instruments.

KING KALAKAUA AS A COMPOSER.

Kalakaua's forte seemed to be writing lyrics as he sought the musical guidance of bandmaster Henry Berger in composing many of his works such as Hawaii Ponoi. Seven songs composed by King Kalakaua appear in *Ka Buke O Na Leo Mele Hawaii (1888)* written under the pseudonym of "Figgs" (for reasons known only to the King). Writing in both English and Hawaiian he also composed many chants or mele such as *"Ka Momi" (The Pearl: 1881)* and *"Ke Alii Milimili" (The Cherished One: 1890)*.

Song written by Kalakaua seems to praise the drinking of gin . . . but also refers to a love affair.

KONI AU I KA WAI: (I THROB FOR LIQUID)

"Ho'ohihi kahi mana'o
I ka 'ehu kai o Pua-'ena,
Kai hawanawana i ka la'i la,
I ka la'i wale a'o Wai-a-lua.

Thoughts fancy
The sea spray at Pua-'ena,
Sea whispering in peace,
The peace of Wai-a-lua.

Hui

Chorus

Koni au, koni au i ka wai,
Koni au i ka wai hu'ihu'i.
I ka wai ali'i, 'o ke kini la,
'Olu ai ka nohona o ka la'i.

I throb, I throb for liquid,
I throb for cool liquid,
Royal liquid—gin—
To make life cool and peaceful.

Alia 'oe e ka 'ehu ai
E lelehune nei i ke one,
One hanau o ke kupuna la,
Pu'ili lau li'i o ka
*   uka.*

Wait, O sea sprays
Misting on the sands,
Birthsands of ancestors,
Small-leafed bamboo of the
*   uplands.*

'Akahi ho'i au la 'ike
I na la'i 'elua;
'Elua maua i ka la'i la
Wai kapipi i ka pali.

Finally I have known
Twofold peace;
We two in peace
Liquid sprinkling on the cliff.

Mele Ma'i were composed in praise of the sexual prowess of a highborn person. This one was written for King Kalakau:

KO MA'I HO'EU'EU: (YOUR LIVELY MA'I)

Ko ma'i ho'eu'eu
Ho'ekepue ana'oe—

Ho'ike i ka mea nui
O Halala i ka nuku manu.

'O ka hana ia o Halala—
Ka hapapai Kikala
A'e a ka lawe a'e 'oe
A i pono iho o Halala.

Ko ma'i ho'olalahu,
I kai 'ale Punana mele,
'O ka hope 'oi iho ai
A i pehu ai ko nuku.

Ua pa ki'aha paha,
Ke noenoe mai nei.
Ha'ina mai ka puana:
'O Halala i ka nuku manu.

Your lively ma'i
That you are hiding—

What Halala does—
Raise the hips
And take you
Right below Halala.

Your *ma'i* swells,
Sea swells a nest of songs,
And finally
Your swollen mouth.

Take a drink perhaps,
Foggy then.
Tell the refrain:
Halala and the many birds.

Show the big thing
Halala to the many birds.

Hawaii State Archives

Kalakaua dressed in plain clothes.

Acknowledgments

State Archives, Honolulu.
Bishop Museum, Hawaii.
Hamilton Library, University of Hawaii.
Dr. Niklaus Schweizer of Honolulu.
Sir Robin Mackworth-Young, Librarian, Windsor Castle.
Berkshire, England.
The Sheraton Palace Hotel, San Francisco.
Santa Barbara Public Library.
Claridges Hotel, London.
Staff of Iolani Palace, Honolulu.

This pictorial biography was compiled with generous assistance from the parties mentioned above.

To them and all the other people who encouraged my project with kind words along the way, I extend my heartfelt gratitude.

Kristin Zambucka,
Honolulu,
December 17th, 1982.